LIVE

ICI REPOSE
VINCENT VAN GOGH
1853 - 1890

Fireplace Compendium

Van Gogh Reader

published by
POETMAN RECORDS USA
P.O. Box 200, Lexington, KY 40588

Front & back cover and page 3 paintings by **Michael Johnathon**
Photo of Michael Johnathon page 7 by **Larry Neuzel**

All photos used in this book by permission or public domain. Every effort possible has been made
to track down the source of each one used in WoodSongs 5. The internet has made that process
almost impossible but we are always doing the best we can.

BOOK and COMPACT DISC ISBN:
978-0-578-95249-9
Library of Congress Control:
202191-4530

Special thanks: Gina Mendello, Loretta Sawyer, Bryan Klausing, Clay Pasternack,
Stacey Taylor, Robert Sherman, Diana Brake, Ian Hart, Roger Coleman, Kate Savage,
Ashley Hanna, Lizanne Knott, Seth Tuska, Bill Wence, Martin Guitars, Deering Banjos,
Jen Chapin, Jason Ashcraft, Melissa & the Twins, Bill Goodman, Peter Holmstedt,
my SongFarmer friends, the WoodSongs Crew
... and Vincent.

A book & album by Michael Johnathon

WoodSongs 5
Fireplace Compendium & Van Gogh Reader

"For my part I know nothing with any certainty, but the sight of the stars makes me dream."
Vincent van Gogh

*P*ainters, *A*rtists *&* *P*oets

This book is for the "creatives," those who birth into reality what the mind says does not exist. They are the poets, painters, dreamers and time travelers, world-wanderers and highway vagabonds, rail riders and drifters. They dream what is unseen so others can appreciate what has been created. They are 5-string politicians, 6-string therapists, banjo barristers, acoustic lovers and penny-pinching peacemakers ... because those who sing together can not fight. They are still there. Still writing, searching, singing, trying to get this world in tune.

One of the biggest under-the-radar tales in all the arts is the backstory of Vincent van Gogh. He was living in a small village in France, up early every morning, painting all day, returning to his tiny apartment above a café where he would have dinner each evening at the same time. A borderline alcoholic, struggling with psychotic episodes, ingesting yellow paint and drinking gallons of coffee he struggled with his health. He was consumed with painting, finishing nearly 3 completed canvases every day.

He was a passionate man, given to a strict schedule, you could almost set your clock to his movements. He loved to read, virtually a scholar of other artists and art. Vincent spoke four languages. And he didn't give up. Ever.

Much like the community of artists today.

But what is happening to all these hard working, struggling musicians, poets, dreamers and wandering souls that make their way across the ribbons of America's highways, trying to sing, scratch out a living with their songs, paintings and poetry?

The creative universe has entered a strange vortex, an empty, confusing digital shadow of what it used to be. They have become *Vincent* searching the world for *Theo, Pete* looking for *Toshi*. I will explain that as you read this book, written in the afterglow of Vincent van Gogh, his brilliant work and even more amazing, too brief life.

Today, our painters, poets and songwriters are drowning in a cyber-tsunami of ones and zeros, streaming their souls across cell phones and iPads for free in such massive volume the odds of hearing them, seeing them is almost nonexistent. And yet they continue to labor in the silence of this digital thundercloud, hoping their work will be found, heard, appreciated, noticed ... maybe even pay their rent.

In these pages I will tell you remarkable stories about several artists who stood strong against the winds of denial and critics. I hope to explain in spirit, common sense and reality how we can all travel through this new world in a way that adds value and purpose to your art, music and passions.

Tout 'a Toi & Folk on,

Folksinger, Painter,
SongFarmer & Tree Hugger
michael@woodsongs.com

"Everything you can imagine is real."
Pablo Picasso

For all artists who struggle in silence,
painting outside the lines & creating for a living.

"Art is what you make others see."
Edgar Degas

"No one buys my paintings."
Vincent van Gogh
(His painting "IRISES" was sold in 1987 for $53 million)

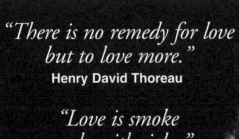

*"There is no remedy for love
but to love more."*
Henry David Thoreau

*"Love is smoke
made with sighs."*
William Shakespeare

*There is nothing more truly
artistic than to love."*
Vincent van Gogh

Dedicated to the life, work, and passion of
Vincent van Gogh

An original oil painting by
MICHAEL JOHNATHON

"I gave my heart to the Banjo"
Pete Seeger

"I put my heart and soul into my work,
and I have lost my mind in the process."
Vincent Willem van Gogh

He was the second
Vincent

"Art is created by the hand of God,
written upon the tablet of the human heart and
released into the world on the wings of a dream."

He was named after his older brother, the first born child of his parents, who died at birth. His mother longed for the first Vincent, so the next Vincent was never able to find who he was in the eyes of his own parents. His father demanded he enter the priesthood, but he failed at that effort. So as a compromise he became a lay minister and worked among the poor and downtrodden. Even then, he was kicked out.

His mother was a painter who enjoyed the exactness of Rembrandt, Michelangelo and other fine artists. When her son decided to become an artist with the help of his brother, Theo, the paintings of his first few years reflected the darkness and depression of what he experienced in his ministry.

His mother was not a fan of his artwork, and his father was disappointed at his career choice.

His first paintings, like *The Weavers* shown above, completed in 1884, are dark, dismal and brown. It reflected the sadness and depression he felt after his ministry. It would be years before he found the light.

Once he moved to France he experienced the energy of color, sunshine, flowers and starry skies. The more he painted, the thicker his paint became and the brighter his color choices were.

During the summer of 1890, his canvases were reflecting incredible energy of yellow, orange and red. His mood was energized by the brightness of light around him. That's one of the reasons I find it very hard to accept that he committed suicide. His paintings reflected a very positive, energetic momentum. His paintings were no longer dark and sad.

During the summer of 1890 he painted one of his most vivid canvases, a field of red poppies in France. Only someone whose heart was full of joy and love of life could paint something this beautiful. In nine weeks, from May through July 1890, Van Gogh produced a breathtaking 106 finished works while living in the small town of Auvers, France.

He was at the height of his creative power, soon to be wasted by a single bullet.

Poppy Field, 1890

Lonely

First Steps, 1890

He never married and had trouble maintaining romantic relationships. From time to time he would write his brother Theo about a lady friend or a girl that he was interested in, but for the most part Vincent van Gogh lived alone.

He filled his loneliness with his dream of becoming a great artist. He worked hard at it. But like many of the girls he was interested in, the world of art rejected him like a spurned lover. He loved several women from afar without approaching them, and he loved the world of art from afar as well.

It seems Vincent had a big heart, and early in his adulthood he tried hard to be a minister who tended the physical and spiritual needs of the downtrodden. When he decided to become a painter, his first works of art were of the struggling and poverty stricken people that he met in his ministry.

But his emotions were unstable and as deeply as he felt for others he struggled with an inner temperament and rage that he had a hard time controlling. He lost as many friends as he made. And very few women could tolerate his mood swings.

In one of the most endearing, tender and sensitive of the nearly 1000 canvases that he painted in a short career, is this painting of a child's first step toward a loving and surprised father tending his garden.

It's a painting that had to have been formed out of Vincent's imagination, as there was no way for this to have been posed for him. It would've had to come from the deep well of his spirit and his heart, the cavernous pool of loneliness that he felt in his spirit. You can almost feel his longing, wishing the man in the painting could have been him.

There's no record of Vincent ever having a child, and he never married. His loneliness became part of one of the greatest stories in the world of art, but it must've been a very painful thing for him to have lived through.

All art is born of isolation, and all artists have an inner loneliness that is often silently hidden. They long for companionship and love, they long for a supportive relationship. Vincent never had that, except for his brother Theo. He was spurned by his artist mother, his family, his friends and many of his fellow painters.

I think many can relate to his inner pain, especially now. This has been a lonely and isolated time, rife with stress and insecurity. Millions lost their jobs, millions have been affected by a tempestuous virus, millions of families have been ripped apart with insecurity. America just might be one of the loneliest nations on earth right now.

"First Steps" was painted in January 1890. Vincent was only 37 years old. He only had a few months left to live.

"My uncle has seen my work
and he thinks it's frightful."
Vincent van Gogh

The Nature of
ART

Art is quiet and shy as it screams to you.

It is a demure woman hiding in the shadows
too beautiful to be revealed,
too insecure to stand in control.

Art is a flower buried in the concrete seeking the sun,
a thunder cloud withholding it treasures
as it lingers above the desert.

Art is a coin of no apparent value that can
still purchase the essence of your soul.

Art demands to be pondered, to be considered,
to be stared at, to be imagined, to cause confusion
as it points toward resolution.

Art is more elegant than the background,
demands to rise above the bottom
and transcends the transparent.

Art is the collision of stars
landing gently on your heart.

*"Art is a lie that
makes us realize the Truth."*
Pablo Picasso

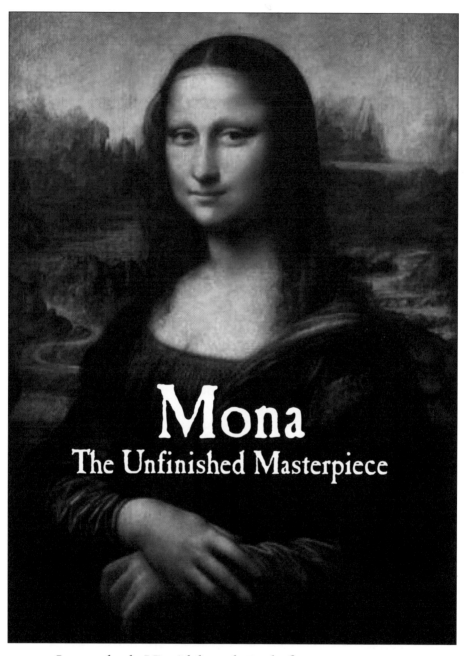

Mona
The Unfinished Masterpiece

Leonardo da Vinci labored nearly four years to create what has become the most valuable painting in world history.

The *Mona Lisa* brush strokes are so fine they are barely discernible when viewed in person. The attention to detail is astounding, almost photographic.

It is assumed da Vinci continued to work on the painting, never satisfied that he was finished with it, for another decade. The portrait is not done on canvas but on poplar wood, another unique fact of the painting.

He had this frustrating and notorious habit of leaving his work unfinished so he could move on to the next project.

One confusing aspect of the Mona Lisa painting is when a historian of da Vinci's day wrote about the portrait, praising it's impeccable detail, explaining how even the *"eyebrows of the portrait are made with the finest brushes."* Yet the Mona Lisa of today has no discernible eyebrows. There is a theory that there were two Mona Lisas, one of them lost.

Leonardo da Vinci
self portrait sketch

What is most amazing about this incredible painting is that da Vinci left it, in his mind, unfinished before he died and he never delivered the painting to the man who commissioned it. Even more incredible ... till this day it is assumed da Vinci was never even paid for his work.

In spite of that, the insured value of the Mona Lisa ... unfinished and all ... is $1 billion.

"Art is never finished ... only abandoned."
Leonardo da Vinci

The Nazi Problem

This is the painting of the Dr. Gachet, Vincent's friend and doctor. Gachet was with Vincent when he died, as was his brother Theo. After Vincent died the painting was eventually sold by Johanna for a paltry 300 francs (just $326 US)

Around 1911 it was purchased by a German collector but later banned by the Nazis. It then passed through the hands of another Nazi, Hermann Goering and, after the war, ended up in the United States with a private collector.

In 1990 it was auctioned for $82 million, sold to a Japanese businessman who intended to burn the painting when he died. Instead it thankfully sold again to an anonymous buyer. The painting remains missing to this day.

The Brother's Wife

Since I brought her up, let's talk about Johanna ... with all the admiration for Vincent's brother, it wasn't *him* that made those paintings so famous and valuable. It was *her,* Theo's wife.

It's true, Theo believed in Vincent, he worked so hard, he stayed so loyal and supported his brother to paint.

Before Vincent died, he and Theo had bitter arguments. Theo was leaving his job at the Gallery to start his own and could not support his brother much longer. Joanna was resenting Vincent because he was a great drain on Theo's finances, she was getting very frustrated and angry.

Plus, Theo was not well. He died from syphilis just months after he held Vincent as he died in the yellow house from the gunshot wound. Johanna watched her husband die in the shadow of his unlikable, unsellable brother. She was left with a small apartment in Paris, a young child to support, no money, a few items of furniture and over 200 valueless works of her dead brother-in-law. Yet, she refused to dispose of them, and was publicly ridiculed for hanging on to such worthless, amateur and ridiculous pieces of art.

It took her 10 years, but she finally convinced a gallery owner to present Vincent's paintings. 10 years of near poverty and she kept all of those rolled up canvases until she could find someone to show them properly. 10 long years ... and when she did, the name of *Vincent van Gogh* became legend. It was Joanna that turned him into a worldwide superstar of the arts. It was Joanna that gave Vincent his reputation. It was Theo's wife, the one who resented Vincent so much, that turned all of those rolled up canvases into precious treasure.

It was Joanna that took the huge volume of letters between the brothers, editing them and found a publisher to print them as a book. It was Joanna that was the caretaker of the legend we know as Vincent van Gogh.

And it was Joanna that dug up her husband Theo's body so that he could be buried alongside his beloved Vincent.

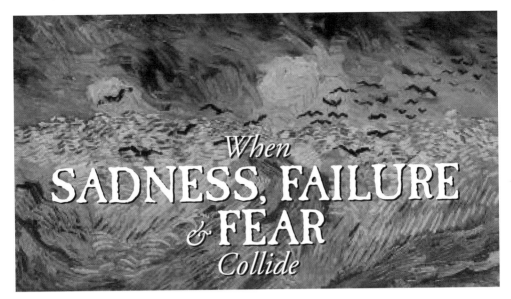

When SADNESS, FAILURE & FEAR Collide

It was Summer, 1890. The relationship between Vincent and his brother Theo, who was financially supporting him for over almost ten years, was about to change.

Vincent felt alarmed by Theo's plan to open an art gallery of his own. On top of his general sense of failure, it meant his future was now uncertain - his brother would be less able to look out for him. His career as a failed artist was certain to end.

Two days after Vincent's death on July 29. 1890, Theo wrote to their mother: *"If he could have seen how people behaved toward me when he had left us and the sympathy of so many."*

In less than six months, Theo would also pass, leaving Johanna alone with hundreds of unmarketable paintings.

Here is one of Vincent's final works, painted the summer of 1890. It was thought to be his last but it has been since discovered that it was probably second or third to his final canvas. It is dark and brooding, stormy and brilliant.

Worth tens of millions today, he could not find a buyer for it. When Johanna finally convinced a gallery in Paris to show some of the paintings, Vincent quickly became a superstar, validating Theo's faith in his brother.

Love, Front Porches and Cancel Culture

Our culture has changed dramatically over the past several years, it's almost unrecognizable from just a generation ago. It seems the spirit of the American front porch has surrendered to the digital septic tank of social media.

Cancel culture has become a way of life. We have become conditioned to "unfriend" each other, to dismiss each other, hang up on someone if you don't like what they say instead of learning how to discuss our differences.

We amputate, isolate, disassociate and eliminate. All in an effort to suspend personal responsibility to maintain friendships and relationships. We claim we have boundaries but use them as emotional walls to prevent access to our emotions.

Isolation and suspension of communication is one of the cruelest actions we can do to each other, fed by a global wave of narcissism not experienced in human history as it is today.

We would rather dig up a misstatement from years ago to condemn people than acknowledge the great effort of good they accomplish in their day-to-day life. Those who are not qualified to judge anything at all judge others harshly as though they know what they're talking about.

Love has become a cliché, a rarely used word that has become mercenary in meaning. That which defines humanity is losing its definition.

Songs have become generic dribble because nobody wants to say anything that might potentially be offensive, politically incorrect, not "woke" enough. Imagine all the songs that would be canceled from the library of music because they don't meet up with the current standards. It is almost shameful.

Taking the lead, sticking your neck out, standing up for a cause has become a dangerous career-threatening enterprise because the risk of being decimated by a misguided opinion has become very real.

The impulse is to condemn, the knee-jerk reaction is to engage in verbal combat all because we don't like somebody else's viewpoint, a different opinion, alternate lifestyle. We preach "freedom" ... so long is that freedom is used in a way that we approve. None of that makes sense.

Buried in this cesspool of cancel culture is the sincere, needed effort to adjust the wrongs of the past. That is a good thing, and that is not necessarily "cancel culture." It is a delicate dance of intention, difficult to navigate and hard to differentiate from one from another.

Never before has the human culture been in desperate need of love and the spirit of the front porch ... And how sad that someone who tries to talk about it is defined as a "snake oil salesman" by those unable to understand the spirit implied.

It is an odd time in history, and it looks like we are in for one heck of a ride. Buckle up, kids. The roller coaster hasn't quite reached the top yet and it will be a long, fast ride down.

*"It's a very important thing to learn
to talk to people you disagree with."*
Pete Seeger

They made him sit on the
BIBLE

It was 1944 in Alcolu, South Carolina. He was a young black boy, just 14 years old and barely 5 feet tall. He weighed less than 100 pounds and, in a jury trial that lasted a mere two hours, he was convicted of killing two young girls and sentenced to death in the electric chair.

Barely a teenager, scared, and alone he walked to the electric chair after being given ice cream by the very guards who would kill him in a few minutes, carrying a family Bible under his arm.

But young George Stinney was too small for the electric chair. His thin, trembling frame wasn't big enough for the helmet carrying the charge that would take his life.

So they made him sit on the Bible so his head would reach the terminals that would kill him, the youngest person in America convicted with the death penalty. He was just a kid.

They made him sit on the very Bible he believed in after the jury deliberated only 10 minutes and that's all it took to take his life, his family, his friends and his future away.

Seventy years later, he was found innocent and his conviction was overturned. But it was too late. During the execution the helmet fell off because he was so small. He suffered with electricity surging through his body several times before he finally died.

And they made him sit on a damn Bible.

A frightened George Stinney before being escorted to the electric chair

Love *has a* Price

This is advice to every creative person: one of the finest lifestyles to have is that of an artist, songwriter, musician, painter, poet. It is a difficult, peaceful, intriguing and fascinating way to make a living. So long as you're *not* in it for the money. You have to be in it for the *love*. Only a passionate belief and love of the art can help you rise above the incredible waves of negativity and discouragement that come along with the lifestyle.

I have also learned first-hand that one of the best things, generous things, for any artist to learn how to do is present other artists. It makes you better ... better on tour and better on stage and better in person. It makes you empathetic to what those who are helping you actually go through.

Learning how to share the stage and widen the spotlight to include others is one of the best ways artists as a community can help each other survive through this ever-changing downturn of what once was the music business.

The danger in that kind of generosity is that your support of other artists will cause many to stop viewing you as an artist. They start thinking you as a presenter, which is something you are not. You're just being helpful, supportive. It is a frustrating dichotomy of intent, being generous of spirit can rob you of your own artistic privilege. And living.

The only way to supersede the wrong impression is to work two times, five times, ten times harder as an artist, songwriter, musician, author or anything else you're trying to do.

"Your profession is not what money gives you,
but what you have come to do on earth with passion."
Vincent van Gogh

The Starry Night

An artist's prayer to nobody.

It is one of the most recognized paintings in the world. Images of *The Starry Night* are everywhere ... on coffee, mugs, prints, t-shirts, towels, magnets. Honestly, it sometimes feels as if the painting's fame has exceeded that of its creator.

Very few realize the intense, lonely and emotional time Vincent was having when this painting was completed. He was living in an insane asylum, by choice, struggling with epileptic fits and periods of extreme depression ... his behavior was erratic, becoming dangerous and it scared him. And others.

From his room in the asylum he would look through the bars to the starlit skies above and struggle with the idea of prayer to a God that he wasn't sure was even there anymore.

Ten years earlier he was part of the ministry, and when he left to become a painter his colors were dark and brooding. When he moved to the south of France he discovered what he called the light and began using vivid, bright colors in his paintings.

But for this relatively small canvas, barely 3' wide, he returned to the dark, pensive shades of his earlier work. *The Starry Night* can be best described as a dream, a wish.

In reality, a prayer.

His usual work habit was to paint from actual life, actual landscapes, actual models. But *The Starry Night* was born completely out of Vincent's imagination. The church steeple and the homes at the bottom of the painting are not real, the swirling, exploding stars are filled with an energy he did not actually see, he just wished it.

But the imagery of his dreams for this painting, a canvas nobody wanted, a painting he could neither give away as a gift nor find a buyer for, is now worth $1 billion and is the most treasured, duplicated, and reproduced painting in the world. Born by a very lonely man living in an insane asylum in France, looking out his window at night and painting his dream during the day.

It was the summer of 1889, and Vincent had less than one year remaining to live.

The Starry Night and a close up of his brush strokes

*"The best way to know God is to love many things.
Art is to console those who are broken by life."*
Vincent van Gogh

She Persisted

Most often an artist must carry their own ball up the hill, no matter how heavy. It's not fun, sometimes it hurts. Almost always it is exhausting.

This lady wasn't known for her intelligence or her vision, she was viewed as a goofy, minor, insignificant partner to her husband who "allowed" her to be part of his productions. Behind the scenes, however, she had a very strong sense of what the audience would respond to, she had a very intuitive perspective on adventurous productions.

One day she was handed a script that nobody liked, and she read it for that reason. And she loved it. She wanted to see this script turn into reality but nobody would help her. Even her big-shot producer husband laughed at the idea. She fought the studios, she battled executives, she argued for the financing.

When all else failed, in the depths of defeat but still believing completely this was a worthy idea, she paid for the pilot to be filmed out of her own pocket. Because her heart was in it, her soul was in it, she just *knew* it would be good. She *knew* it would work.

And that is how Lucille Ball got the TV series *Star Trek* made ...

... and *The Andy Griffith Show, The Untouchables, The Dick Van Dyke Show* and more.

"I can't change the fact that my paintings don't sell. But the time will come when people will recognize that they are worth more than the value of the paints used in the picture."
Vincent van Gogh

Energy, Apathy, The Peter Principle and The Music Business

Life is like a Coin, there are just so many nickels in the bank and they will get spent with or without your participation. When you are in the arts, the wise use of those coins is to be as productive, energetic and diverse as possible.

The problem, from my experience, is anyone with the motivation to explore their art and life to its fullest will be met by severe opposition, even outright disdain, by those who not only can't accomplish that much, but are incapable of understanding how you are even able to do it. In a word: they are jealous.

"How do you get so much done? How are you so fast? How do you organize this?" And while they waste time commiserating the volume and value of what you did, you go to work and come out with the next project.

Somebody once told me that leaving others in a cloud of dust also leaves them in a cloud of confusion. To validate their failure, those who *can't* will condemn those who *can* ... because your success bothers them. More often than not those in the position of authority, those who have achieved a level of accomplishment got there because they are not qualified to go any further. Years ago that was called, the *Peter Principle* ... when someone reaches their level of total incompetence.

> *"Society often forgives the criminal*
> *but never the dreamer."*
> **Oscar Wilde**

The same with critics. Good Lord, I've seen it happen over and over and over again. And it is a shame because the world of the arts should be full of support, unity and sense of community. We should be cheering each other on.

The depth of your despair is the template, the canvas for your masterpiece. Do not underestimate the creative power of your broken heart. The criticism of those who have reached the limits of their creative incompetence becomes your fuel.

Press down the pedal of your heart and roar to the finish line. My advice to all those who hear the clock of life ticking away, who look at the breadth of their opportunities, who want to use the brightest and boldest colors, who see their music as more than just selling a CD but actually moving others to some kind of action:

Don't just think outside the box,
use your creative energy to crush the box
and create a brand new one.

Depend on no one. Roll your own ball up the hill with pride and dignity. Ignore the critics incapable of doing what you are accomplishing. Never take their apathy personally, view it as validation of your accomplishments and energy. They don't understand how it's done and you're pissing them off.

Spend your coins in the bank of life as wisely as possible and leave behind a legacy of good work. The only comment we should make on our last breath is:

"I can't believe I did all that."

"In spite of everything, I shall rise again;
I will take up my brush, forsaken in my great discouragement,
and I will go on with my painting."
Vincent van Gogh

Black Lines Matter

One of the things that made the style of Vincent so unique and rare was his habit of outlining the images of his paintings. Much like a cartoonist would do today, he would use black lines to make the images leap off the canvas.

It was also one of the reasons patrons and gallery owners refused to support his art. To them it looked lazy and childish, yet today it is revered, duplicated and worth millions.

Here is an example, *Noon - Rest from Work (after Millet)*. You can see the generous use of black in the outlines. His technique was not by accident, it was by design even though the community of artists and patrons completely rejected his style.

Every masterpiece so valued today, from *The Starry Night* to *Sunflowers* was considered amateur and of no merit, worthy only of ridicule. But he never gave up, he never quit, he never stopped trying.

*"A great fire burns within me,
but no one stops to warm themselves at it,
and passers-by only see a wisp of smoke."*

Vincent van Gogh

Theo & Toshi

Greatness is never achieved alone. It is built up by the belief, support and good wishes of, usually, one other person.

Vincent had his younger brother Theo, who encouraged and supported him. He paid for all of Vincent's paint supplies and sent him money to live on even though he himself was not a wealthy man. He worked in galleries and tried his best to sell Vincent's work but only managed one sale during his brother's brief career. Shortly after Vincent's passing, Theo himself succumbed to syphilis and it was left up to Theo's wife, Johanna, to introduce Vincent's artwork to the world.

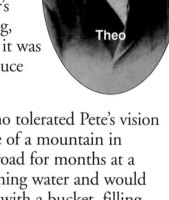

Theo

Pete Seeger had his wife Toshi, who tolerated Pete's vision of building his own log cabin on the side of a mountain in Beacon, NY. While he was gone on the road for months at a time she raised her children with no running water and would walk down the mountainside to a brook with a bucket, filling the pail and walking back to the rustic cabin, heated only by a fireplace in winter.

Without Theo, there is no Vincent van Gogh. Without Toshi, there is no Pete Seeger.

I'm sure there were times when Theo looked at his brother's paintings and thought they were absolutely terrible. I'm sure when Pete came home one night and said, *"I want to build a boat and sail it up and down the Hudson River,"* her first reaction might've been looking in the Yellow Pages for a divorce attorney.

You may not be the artist, but do not underestimate the powerful role you play in supporting the visionary in your midst. Theo and Toshi have gone down in history bathed in the radiant glory of the one they supported.

The Truth about Toshi

More than one have made a comment reflecting some misunderstanding about Pete Seeger's wife. So I thought I would give my viewpoint:

Toshi Seeger had a backbone of iron and the will of Pennsylvania steel. Any suggestion that Toshi was a humble, meek, subservient person who did what she was told at the sacrifice of her own dreams is *highly* inaccurate.

Let's set the record straight, Toshi was a determined, highly motivated, extremely intelligent woman who took no orders from anybody. Not even Pete. I think it can be fairly said from anyone who knew her, she was Pete's superior in many ways, and he knew it.

Toshi loved being a mother, loved being a wife, loved to cook and garden. She enjoyed filmmaking and pottery.

In many ways, even more than Harold Leventhal, she was Pete's agent and manager. She made decisions on his behalf, when he got involved in a cause or project, she would often manage and steer the idea to success.

When the sloop *Clearwater* was ready to launch in Maine, they had to come up with the money to pay the builder before it could leave the dock. It was Toshi who got on the phone and raised $50,000 to get the Clearwater out to sea.

Toshi chose her lifestyle with clarity. She enjoyed being shoulder to shoulder to Pete, she was never in his shadow, just not in the spotlight. Anyone who knew her personally would know as a point of fact that Toshi never did anything she did not absolutely want to be part of. End of story.

Pete and Toshi had a magnificent partnership, and Pete was well aware of her value. The world would not have Pete Seeger had it not been for Toshi, and somehow that is interpreted as her accepting a subservient role.

If you knew her, you would know how wrong that was.

Would her life have been different if she pursued her own interests as a sole goal? Probably so. But she did not want that. Would Theo's life have been different if he focused on a more successful artist other than his brother Vincent? No doubt that would be true as well. But Theo did not want that.

The world knows who Toshi and Theo are because of the great gift they gave us in supporting someone they loved deeply. Perhaps their journey could have been different ... but they did not want that journey.

Toshi and Theo were not the ones living in the spotlight but their love, loyalty and counsel gave them a place in history ... it made them both honored, deeply admired and legendary.

*"I don't really have any friends except for you,
and when I'm ill you're always in my thoughts."*
Vincent to his brother Theo

The Peace Keeping Army

I see several social movements growing, some organized, some grassroots, and many political. I see organizations on the left aiming political rifles at groups on the right, and I see groups on the right aiming political shotguns at organizations on the left but I don't see them doing anything to help their communities as a whole. I see a lot of noise, angst and lost friendships, but not many positive actions that actually do helpful things for anyone.

So, I cast my lot with the true peacekeepers of the earth. Those who plant gardens, raise their families, support their neighbors and welcome friends to their front porches. The poets, artists, dreamers and playwrights, the songwriters and visionaries working in the silence of their anonymous life.

They are the greatest peacekeeping force in the history of mankind. The arts are valuable because artists get people to stop. Get them to stand quietly. And listen. It's physically impossible to fight during the act of listening and that is what musicians, writers, poets and artists of all kinds do for planet earth. They get people to stop… And listen.

Art and songs are important, they are vital and necessary. There's a reason the book of Psalms, a book of song lyrics, is the biggest book of the Bible. Stand with the peacekeepers during a time of unrest. Do what you can to turn your front porch into the grand stage of your hometown. Be one of the creative artists who help your family and neighbors to stop.

And listen.

*"In a world of Peace and Love
music would be the universal language."*
Henry David Thoreau

Norman

One of the greatest American artists in the 20th century never considered himself an "artist," he would only refer to himself as an *illustrator.*

He felt a true artist was well above his personal abilities and career choices. He deemed himself too commercial to be a real artist and he was very self conscious about how he over marketed his paintings. Be that as it may, he was one of the most prolific and exceptional painters of the last hundred years. And certainly among the most successful.

There is no way I could ever aspire to come close to his style and attention to detail. What I do admire greatly is his studio space in Stockbridge MA. It is now part of a museum in tribute to his career and I look forward to visiting someday.

Here is Norman Rockwell, the *artist,* in his studio.

Coffin Nails

Vincent wasn't exactly a health nut. He rarely bathed, drank too much, had a horrible diet and consumed huge amounts of booze and coffee.

And he smoked. Although later in life he preferred a pipe, he was also one to roll a cigarette. In 1886 he had an odd compulsion to do an oil painting of a skull smoking. No kidding, this is an actual van Gogh.

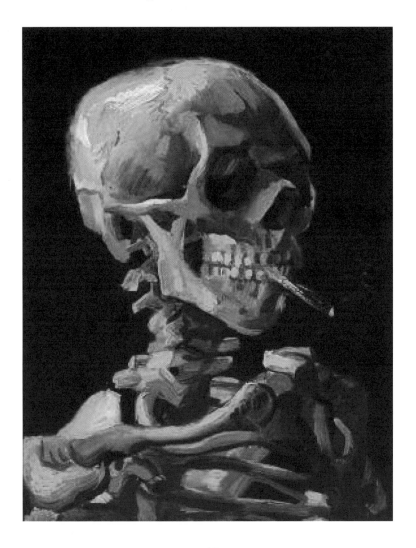

Whistler's Mom

It is prized as America's own *Mona Lisa,* yet the portrait of the woman sitting in profile was, in a word, a mistake.

James McNeill Whistler, an American artist living in England was doing a study he referred to as an "arrangement," not a portrait. His usual model could not make it on this certain day and so he got his mother, Anna, to stand in her place.

His mother was uncomfortable standing so, at the last minute, James decided she could be seated.

When it was was completed he presented it to the London Arts Academy for a gallery display. It was a large canvas, about 60x60" with his own home made frame. Sadly, members of the Academy *hated* the painting and it was eventually accepted only by default. This infuriated Whistler and he resented the Academy for the prejudice against his work.

Broke, he eventually pawned the painting to raise cash. Once that happened the painting suddenly gained new life and made its way to Paris, where it was held in very high esteem.

Using mostly blacks and grays, the painting of *Whistler's Mother* is unique among American paintings, serving as a template for other American artists like Norman Rockwell.

Hated by one, valued by another ... so it is with great art. Today it is one of the most valuable paintings in the world.

Speaking of Mommy

Van Gogh had a strained and contentious relationship with his mother, due in part because her first born child, also named Vincent, died at birth. Our Vincent came later and his mom always resented him because of the death of the first child.

He lived in the shadow of his dead brother, so he became very close to his younger sibling, Theo, who financially supported his all too brief career as an artist.

His mother was also an artist and she did not approve of Vincent's style, his choices, his work and was very disappointed when he left the ministry. Actually, she hated Vincent's artwork. She made it clear to all she was very ashamed of her son. She was the seed of his isolation and loneliness for the rest of his life.

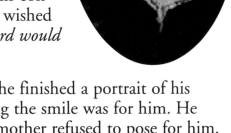

One of Vincent's letters to Theo implied he would bring his canvases to his mother's home and she would use his drawings and paintings to fix the holes in her goat barn. Can you imagine?

When Vincent fell ill and went into the asylum, his mother wrote to Theo that she was humiliated by Vincent and was burdened by his constant needs. She wrote how she wished Vincent would die, and *"the Lord would take him."*

The year before he died he finished a portrait of his smiling mother, perhaps wishing the smile was for him. He used an old photo because his mother refused to pose for him.

"The sadness will last forever."
Vincent van Gogh

37

Finding Michelangelo

The Roman Empire's grip on the world began to crumble, so a grand political move was devised as a desperate effort to maintain control: Rome would use religion as a political force.

Called the *"Council of Nicaea,"* in 325 A.D. several decisions were made to pull the collapsing empire together. Beliefs from various parts of the world were reassembled into one common doctrine. This is where pagan customs like Christmas, Easter, the Trinity and other traditions became accepted as christian. This political gathering of religious beliefs across the empire was called *conmunis* in Latin, in Greek *catholicus,* or in English *Catholic.*

Christianity was unified with paganism, so the Phoenician worship of sex was merged with Easter, the birth of Christ was moved from October to December, the Babylonian and southern Asian concept of a triad God became the trinity and so on.

It was at this counsel where permission was finally granted so artists could portray the faces of God, the Christ and angels. Before this, many were executed for their offenses. Sound familiar?

It is considered one of the most important decisions for the arts in human history, without which the works of Rembrandt, Michelangelo and da Vinci would never have happened.

Rage, Riots, Racism and the Arts

What should artists do when society around them seems to be unraveling?

In my home state of Kentucky, riots erupted in protest over the killing of 26 year old medical technician, Breonna Taylor. It happened shortly after midnight during a drug raid at her home. She was shot eight times ... and no drugs were found in her apartment.

In Minneapolis, a policemen pressed his knee on the neck a black man who begged for help until he died. City after city, America erupted in rightful protest, followed by riots and massive looting of innocent store owners, overshadowing the tragedy of George Floyd.

A virus needs a host to exist. So does hate and racism.

I am not going to sit in judgment over anyone in these sad events because I wasn't there, didn't see it happen, and can't place myself in the shoes of those who did. But I don't like it. When someone loses their life for any reason it is heartbreaking. They are gone. They lost their privilege of seeking justice or apologizing, making restitution or demanding fairness.

I am weary of hearing of black men begging to breathe. And I am tired of our officers in blue being harmed and killed.

"We've learned to fly the air as birds,
We've learned to swim the sea as fish
Yet we haven't learned to walk the Earth
as brothers and sisters"
Martin Luther King Jr

Social distancing, isolation and the economic collapse with millions of Americans losing their jobs caused the fabric of our society to rip apart. People's nerves are still on edge. They are anxious and I fear many are using terrible events as an excuse to be angry, not to actually solve anything. We went from the greatest economy on earth to hundreds of thousands of Americans standing on food lines ... in mere months. Our world is changing before our very eyes. It seems so unsolvable.

Yet, every generation had their "standing on the precipice of disaster" moment, when everything seemed hopeless and doomed, but they recovered. For example:

In 1865 the country was torn apart in civil war, hundreds of thousands of young men killed in battle and the President was shot. It seemed so horrible, unrecoverable.

But it did.

In 1918 we were ravaged by the first World War. Over 20 million people died in a global bloodbath followed by the Spanish flu, killing another 20 million. It seemed unrecoverable.

But it did.

Then in 1929 the stock market crashed sending the nations of the earth into a deep depression, setting the stage for the rise of Hitler, which in turn plunged the world into another global conflict. World War II was a tsunami of death, the deadliest conflict in human history with nearly 85 million people losing their lives ... forever. More than half of those killed were innocent civilians, many of whom died because of deliberate genocide, massacres, mass-bombings, disease, and starvation. Over what? Why? The world seemed unhealable.

But it did.

In 1963 Kennedy was murdered in front of tens of millions on TV. It was shocking. Horrible. Unbelievable. How could the nation recover? Yet a few months later *The Beatles* landed in America and everything changed.

World Wars, Korea, Vietnam, Watergate, Aids, 9/11 ... each time it seemed hopeless. Unrecoverable. We will never laugh and sing again, right?

But we did. Each time.

Post Covid-19 and the unrest that came with it. We are witnessing the most massive transfer of wealth in the history of mankind ... and between money, politics and the polarization of the news media I can't tell what is true and what is exaggerated.

All I know is John Prine is gone, and so are untold others around the world from this thing.

"Music was my refuge.
I could crawl into the space between the notes
and curl my back to loneliness."
Maya Angelo

Each time the world looked like it was falling apart, great art and music was created. Darkness makes light powerful, and art is light against the dark stormy clouds of life.

During the Civil War, artists like Henry David Thoreau, Vincent van Gogh and Mark Twain stared a world covered in a blanket of evil straight in the eyes and created some of mankind's most beloved works.

During WW1, George Gershwin envisioned an opera about black people at a time of great prejudice. The production was a disaster, but *Porgy & Bess* led by the aria *Summertime* has become one of the most performed operas in America.

During WW2 and in the shadow of massive dust storms a scrappy, eternally unemployed fellow from Oklahoma wrote a simple song that is still being sung by millions, as Woody Guthrie turned the disaster of war and climate change into brilliant art.

Art is born of isolation, it is that quiet silence that creates the biggest, boldest and loudest noise. We are in a moment of isolation, a moment of history that is not on the precipice of disaster ... but of great art. Brilliant music. Powerful poetry and literary greatness.

I suppose it all comes down to perspective. We are not falling off the cliff, we are standing on the edge of greatness, ready to fly across a dark canyon into the arms of brilliant sunlight.

That is the power of art. That is the power of music. That is the role of artists, known and unknown.

> *"A few chords strummed on a ukulele does more good*
> *in this world than the combined efforts*
> *of every politician that ever lived."*
> **Frank Littig, written shortly after WW1**

A song or painting can not bring Breonna Taylor back. A brilliant novel or sensitive poetry can not give life back to George Floyd, or take away the choking and gasping as he tried to breathe with someone's knee on his neck. But neither can judges, preachers, politicians or lawyers.

Woody Guthrie couldn't change the reality of poor people during the Great Depression ... but he did give them a voice. He did uplift their spirits. He did make them want to move forward.

Nobody sits around quoting the greedy bankers who took advantage of folks back then ... but we sure do sit around our front porches singing Woody Guthrie songs.

Art lasts longer than the problems that inspire art.

George Gershwin couldn't bring 40 million lost souls back to life after WW1, he couldn't cure the ravages of the Spanish Influenza ... but he did create an opportunity that gave voice to black artists with an opera that nobody liked. At the time, anyway.

"Let's turn the clock back to when people lived in small towns and took care of each other."
Pete Seeger

Thus is the role of every artist, songwriter and musician in the wake of Covid-19. You are here to change the world, to keep it going. Your job is to shine light in darkness.

You do that with great art, not by trying to be a "star." You do that with good work, not with a big ego. You do that with humility, hard work and willingness to be ignored.

You do that the same way Van Gogh, Thoreau, Twain, Gershwin, Guthrie and Pete Seeger did it. Art must always be bigger than one's self ... and the artist must always be lesser than the art created. Thoreau didn't stay in a $28 cabin on the shores of Walden Pond for two years, two months and two days because he wanted to be famous. He just wanted to write a book about his beloved brother John. He couldn't find the words, so he wrote about the earth and his love of nature instead.

Henry's simple journals became the book "Walden" ... and changed literary history forever. He didn't write it for the fame.

Or money. Or glory. He wrote it because he loved to write and had something important to say. Thoreau didn't know he would change the world, still reeling from civil war.

But he did.

You can, too. Never underestimate the strength of your silence, the fertile garden of your isolation, or the power of your own front porch. Which brings me to the point of this chapter:

People are hurting and angry. When the masses *ignore* authority the masses *become* authority. At a time of unrest, a time of social upheaval, riots and violence, remember the source of the artists' power: *Listening*.

That makes you, my fellow artist - big and small, new and experienced - part of the greatest peace keeping force in history. Yes, it's worth repeating in this book.

Use your power. Now. Write and sing. And help this weary, tired world recover.

""Shhhhh.
Listen to the sound around you.
As light taught Monet to paint,
the earth may be teaching you music."
Pete Seeger

"The earth has music for
those who will listen."
William Shakespeare

"To affect the quality of the day,
that is the highest of arts."
Henry David Thoreau

Starry, Starry Nothing

Shortly before his passing Vincent was invited to display some of his paintings in Brussels. Among the artists in the exhibit with the likes of Renoir and Toulouse Letrec. Vincent sent six paintings including the masterpiece *Iris* and *The Starry Night,* which was inspired by a dream of swirling light and stars. He wrote, *"first I dream my painting, then I paint my dream."*

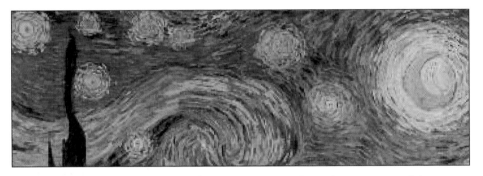

All six paintings were rejected, and nothing was sold.

Sometime later, during an argument with young boys while trying to paint, he was shot in the chest. His brother Theo came quickly to help to Vincent. Lying in bed together as they did as young boys, Theo held his brother close until he passed away at 1:30 in the morning. It took him 30 hours to die.

Six months later, Theo himself died mostly of a broken heart. And syphillis. Theo's wife took it upon herself to continue her husband's work and collect Vincent's paintings. A tavern owner found several paintings and used them for target practice. Vincent's own mother, who hated his artwork, threw out crates and crates of artwork and used many of them to fix the holes in her goat barn.

Today, Vincent and Theo are buried next to each other in a French cemetery. Vincent once wrote to his brother, *"I will never amount to anything as an artist, I just know it."*

The Strangest of Fruit

She went from working in a brothel as a young girl to one of the greatest jazz singers in American music history. Yet, today very few people know anything about her or her music.

Discovered by a very young John Hammond, the same producer who later signed Bob Dylan and Bruce Springsteen, she recorded great songs like *Blue Moon, Embraceable You, I'll Be Seeing You,* and *God Bless the Child.* She was plagued by legal troubles, alcohol and drug abuse. After a short prison sentence, she performed a sold-out concert at Carnegie Hall.

But is was her brave rendition of *Strange Fruit,* an unforgiving, haunting song about racial violence and black people hanging from trees, that caused her to come under constant FBI surveillance for the rest of her days.

She died of alcohol abuse and cirrhosis of the liver after six weeks in a hospital, her room invaded by police as she lay strapped in the bed. This incredible icon of American music supposedly had $750 taped to her leg and only 70 cents in the bank when she died. She was only 44.

Abused, mistreated and overlooked in life, Billie Holiday was later nominated for 23 Grammy awards.

"Success is not final, failure is not fatal.
it is the courage to continue that counts."
Winston Churchill

Loud *but not so* Clear

I find various points of view helpful and sometimes I will post them on social media, not as political statements but simply as ideas of interest. I think all opinions are important and I have no fear of someone who thinks differently than me.

Recently I posted a math professor's economic view of social proposals and their costs weighed against an increase in the minimum wage.

I never said what I personally thought about it, I did not mention any candidate and I did not endorse any particular idea. I simply thought the article was interesting.

You would have thought that I took a deep dive into the *Cesspool of Satan.* The thunderous, dark storms of the digital volcano was deafening ... the raging personal attacks from those drowning in the tsunami of their own assumptions is incredible.

And it reminded me of the state of social freedom. It's almost nonexistent. A personal statement on a personal page has become an open invitation for verbal gunfire, very unpleasant.

A teacher at a regional college, someone whose work I admired and respected, unfriended and blocked me because she assumed I thought a certain way ... she was wrong, I do not ... but she did it without a single personal exchange or conversation.

It seems freedom of speech is allowed only when it agrees with everybody else.

"There is peace even in the storm"
Vincent van Gogh

My John Prine Story

Many moons ago I started a music project called *The Troubadour Concert Series* as a way to bring my friends and artists I admired into my area near Lexington, KY. It was all volunteer, community run and we turned an old movie house into a concert hall once a month or so. It was fun, we thought it would be a great summer project. I was a green kid who didn't know much but somehow convinced Budweiser to sponsor the concert series in a theatre that didn't sell beer. Amazing.

That was over 400 concerts ago and it's still going strong. It was early in the series and, by chance, Al Bunetta called and wanted to have John Prine perform at the Kentucky theater.

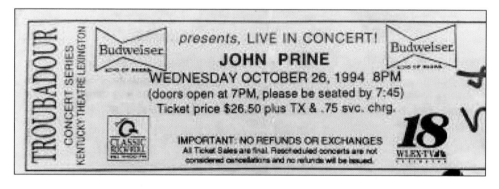

Al was John's manager, a brusque fellow who spoke with the intensity of a northerner, even though he lived in Nashville. We arranged for John to come perform two nights in a row. Both concerts sold out.

Then, a couple days before the concert, a policeman shot a young boy hiding in a closet. Tensions in Lexington were high, especially downtown where the theatre was.

The afternoon of the first concert a riot broke out, people stormed downtown along Main Street, somebody threw a brick through the glass doors of the Kentucky Theater. Police presence was very high ... but John Prine was already in the building.

Outside, police in riot gear with rifles begin running up and down main street. The manager, Fred Mills, got a phone call that said downtown was shutting down. It was 4 PM, and sound check was beginning on stage.

Here was the dilemma: once the artist enters the theatre the contract is in play. In other words, John was getting paid whether the concert happened or not.

I waited for the street to clear a little bit, and ran down the sidewalk to the police department which was only two blocks away. I bolted through the front door and asked the first officer I saw if downtown was really being closed. He said yes. I explained to him we had a sold-out concert at the theater and we had no way of telling the audience not to come. The officer said that was not his problem. I asked who else I might talk to and he told me the only one would be the chief of police.

Frustrated, I walked into the men's room of the police station to clear my head and try to figure out what to do. There, standing 5 feet away from me facing the wall as fellows would do, was the Chief of Police. I told him who I was and what my problem was and he repeated, Lexington is shut down because of the riot.

I told him, *"if you want to see a real riot, tell 800 ticket buyers anxious to see John Prine they can't come to the concert."*

He washed his hands in the sink, looked at me and said, *"all right let me see what I can do."*

Two hours later, with John Prine having dinner backstage, the police in riot gear lined main street, officers up and down from the Kentucky Theater. They escorted the sold out audience into the concert hall for a night with Mr. Prine.

Somewhere in my big boxes of photographs is an unusual picture of me and John Prine. The Kentucky Theatre had an old fashioned box office with no computer. They kept track of ticket sales on a big crayon chart. I'm not kidding. The booking agent and manager wanted documentation of the sold out audience. The only way we could do that was to take a photograph of me, John Prine and Fred Mills holding up the big crayon chart of the Kentucky Theater to prove the sell out.

Well, I searched everywhere and can't find it, but I did find this photo of Troubadour volunteer Rick Rushing with John Prine inside the Kentucky Theatre the day of the riots.

RIP John. I remember you sitting on the couch backstage eating a huge barbecue sandwich having a good laugh about what we went through for that concert to happen that night.

"Writing is about a blank piece of paper and leaving out what's not supposed to be there."
John Prine

Michelangelo 2.0

*"Every block of stone has a statue inside it
and it is the task of the sculptor to discover it."*
Michelangelo

I've been studying with interest *The Sistine Chapel Ceiling* by Michelangelo, an incredible accomplishment. He was born in Florence and, during the early 1500s, became the leading voice in European art worldwide.

It took him four years to paint the 300 intricate images, laying on special scaffolding he designed and built to work on the curved architecture of the chapel.

It was hard work for him. His apprentices mixed his paint, prepared the plaster and moved the massive scaffolding, some were allowed to paint minor things, like sky and clouds. The vast majority was done by Michelangelo himself.

Work was so intense that it damaged his eyesight. He really preferred to work in stone and marble but his prolific nature as an artist drew him to painting every so often.

A separate work from the chapel was his *Conversion of Saul* who later became the apostle Paul. The depiction of light using oils and canvas is absolutely breathtaking

It makes my minor attempts feel so insignificant. Trying to be a painter and then looking over the work of Michelangelo is like playing on your guitar and then listening to Tommy Emmanuel. Art should inspire, not make you want to take your oils, brushes, canvas and easel and hurl them into the woodstove.

"If people knew how hard I worked to get my mastery,
it wouldn't seem so wonderful at all."
Michelangelo c1560

Music, Art & America's Front Porch

It's been a strange few years in America, right? It makes you want to do something to help fix things, but it's hard to figure out the right course to take. Everyone is so polarized and even a simple or kind act is judged through a political prism. It's frustrating.

Community action does not have to be political, sometimes it is done simply in the spirit of love.

Once upon a time, rural communities across America would gather with their neighbors on front porches ... the grand pulpit of hometowns, the gathering place of grandparents, moms, dads and children, neighbors and lemonade in the summertime, front row seats to the sunset and the rising moon.

The music of the front porch is traditionally banjos and fiddles, mandolins and guitars, old songs that everybody knows, grandma singing an ancient ballad to the baby grandchild in her arms on the front porch swing.

As the modern age ascended, our new culture with its air conditioning and television brought people inside behind closed doors ... and the music and comfort of the front porch gave way to the new *feng shui welcome* to homes across suburban landscapes: the garage door.

Compounded by the tsunami impact of the Internet, we have reduced our ability to communicate with each other from the elegance of hand written letters down to personality-free 140 character tweets. To me, the front porch is the emotional symbol of communities bonding together. And I cannot think of another time in history when the bond of the front porch is more needed than right now.

To me, rural areas of the country, like Kentucky, are the fertile birthing ground of America's front porch. It is the gentle rocking chair, the sturdy oakwood of this much-needed front porch. But the front porch spirit matters as much in a New York City highrise as it does in an Indiana farmhouse.

As we watch angry and frustrated neighbors storming capital buildings, venting frustrations, polarizing points of view, condemning each other for how others think, as we watch an entire generation drift farther and farther away from what the front porch represented, the words of Winston Churchill come to mind. When asked by a reporter if he was going to remove the arts from the government budget to support the war effort, Churchill reportedly looked at the news man and bellowed,

"Then what on earth are we fighting for?"

The stress and anxiety between polarized communities was further ignited by a global pandemic and economic turmoil. The uneasiness, insecurity and fear not just of what's going on around us but of what tomorrow is going to bring, is pushing many to the breaking point. Isolation and depression, narcissism and selfishness have become epidemic.

Perhaps this is a time to consider reaching out to what the front porch should represent to all of us. With the music industry in complete disarray and careers of songwriters and performers in near collapse after a lengthy dormancy, perhaps the true purpose of music and art should be re-examined.

The greatest stage in the world is in fact your own front porch. The greatest audience in the world is your own family. The brightest spotlight in the world shines on your living room couch. Home is the greatest venue on earth.

That is why all artists should open up the lens of our collective spotlight to include as many others as possible. It does more to brighten our stage then to jealously keep others away.

Your home, no matter where it might be, is the grand fertile birthing ground of the front porch art form. Perhaps we've drifted so far away from that truth that it is hard to imagine, hard to even believe. But it's become more important than ever for communities to again embrace the gentle power of what has been represented all along by the vanishing front porch.

Once upon a time in Europe there was an old saying that went, *"if everybody in the whole world simply took care of their own homes, you would not have to worry about the world anymore."*

In the 1960s this became a bumper sticker, *"Think globally, act locally."*

It is not just a Kumbaya cliché, but the front porch represents everything that we love about our homes, our communities, our families and our neighbors. Maybe it's time to revisit what the front porch represents ... before the house the front porch belongs to burns down.

"We need a Front Porch 'round the World."
from the song FRONT PORCH

Kerouac & Seven Years

Jack Kerouac leans closer to a radio
to hear himself on a broadcast in 1959.

(John Cohen/Getty Images)

The great American writer, Jack Kerouac, was born in
Massachusetts and raised by Canadian parents. He did not learn
to speak English until he was six years old. In high school he
became a recognized football star but, instead of pursuing sports,
he entered the Merchant Marines during World War II.

After the war he began writing. Between 1949 and 1956
he wrote 12 novels that no publisher was willing to release. He
was considered a literary failure.

In 1951 he started a journal called *On the Road* based on
a friend, Neil Cassidy. He would write on long reams of teletype
paper by hand in pencil instead of using a typewriter.

It took seven long, frustrating years before *On the Road* was belatedly published in 1958. It became instantly recognized as an American masterpiece.

At first, the New York Times published a rave review, comparing Kerouac to Hemingway. Less than two weeks later, the same newspaper changed their mind, attacking the book and calling him, *"a Neanderthal with a typewriter."* Can you imagine?

He was championed, among others, by poet Allen Ginsberg. Jack convinced William Burroughs to start writing and gave him the title of his most famous book, *Naked Lunch.*

Considered a handsome man, he became the darling of the beat generation. Fame and commercial success so rattled him he began drinking heavily and fell into deep despair, crippling depression and became suicidal.

Being Catholic, he knew we couldn't kill himself, so he claimed he would drink himself to death. This he did, literally, and his drunkeness became legendary. He drank until his insides burst from alcohol abuse and died at just 47.

Allen Ginsberg was among the pallbearers at his funeral, and later brought Bob Dylan to visit Jack's graveside, shown here.

"The only truth is music."
Jack Kerouac

Vincent in Love

*"There is nothing more truly
artistic than to love."*
Vincent Van Gogh

Vincent had an emotional relationship with a woman who modeled for several painters of the day. Agostina Segatori was not beautiful woman but an intense and intelligent lady who owned a café. She was the first to give Vincent a gallery showing in Paris.

They started out very affectionate with each other but, as with many of his other friendships, it became stormy and ended badly. In a very selfish act, Agostina was angry and kept many of the van Gogh canvases she had hanging in her café and refused to release them back to Vincent and Theo.

One of the obscure and unknown paintings was his nude portrait of his ex-girlfriend. She affected him deeply and added to his overwhelming sense of loneliness. He reached out to many women but none supported and helped him as Agostina Segatori did. Their relationship ended in 1887.

He had three more years to live.

Vincent, Gauguin ✺ The House of Orgasm

"I am the Holy Spirit; my spirit is whole."

Here is a fascinating look into Vincent's relationship with fellow artist Paul Gauguin. Paul was a gruff, rude, womanizing, obnoxious, perverted French Post-Impressionist artist and, like Vincent, unappreciated until after his death. I wonder why.

Gauguin was eternally broke, like most artists. Nobody liked his paintings. Actually, nobody liked *him*. At 35 years old, he left his job as a tarp salesman in Denmark to become a full-time artist. He abandoned his wife and five children (it is said she was glad to be rid of him) and moved to Tahiti to enjoy the good life of a bachelor. Obsessed with younger women, most of his nudes are of teenagers he had sex with.

He eventually fell deeply in debt and turned to Vincent's brother for help. Theo agreed to try and sell some of Paul's paintings on commission at his gallery.

Part of the arrangement was essentially a bribe, Theo would help him only if he went to live with his brother in France to keep him company. This excited Vincent, the idea of a friend and artist companion was exhilarating, so he spent what little money he had on his modest apartment to make it "as nice as possible" for Paul.

Vincent's dependence on Paul grew into more than just friendship, and van Gogh became obsessed with his fellow painter. Paul resisted his clingy nature, which made Vincent feel rejected. And angry.

Nerves on edge, Vincent began to act strangely. He drank too much absinthe plus huge amounts of coffee, essentially decimating his fragile state.

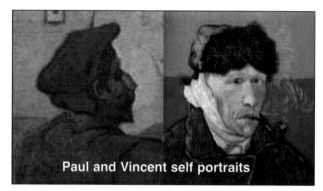
Paul and Vincent self portraits

Gauguin himself later wrote,

"During the latter days of my stay, Vincent would become excessively rough and noisy, and then silent. On several nights I caught him in the act of getting up and coming over to my bed ... It was enough for me to say quite sternly, 'What's the matter with you?' for him to go back to bed without a word."

Another time Vincent crept in Paul's room, laughing madly, and wrote on the wall,

"I am the Holy Spirit; my spirit is whole."

That creeped Paul out, as you can imagine. Eventually their two month relationship became so strained, obnoxious, infuriating and nerve-racking that one night, a wet Christmas Eve's eve, Vincent crept through the darkness to stab Paul with a knife. When Gauguin saw Vincent sneaking from behind, Vincent fled in the darkness and went back to his room and cut a portion of his ear off with the very knife meant for Gauguin. This rattled Paul so much that he decided to leave and break his arrangement with Theo, returning to Tahiti.

Soon after, Vincent entered an asylum for treatment for his depression. The doctors noticed that he was eating his paints and drinking turpentine on top of everything else, making his condition progressively worse.

Far away, Vincent's brother desperately tried to sell some paintings. He would often organize a showing in a gallery but nobody would ever purchase any of Vincent's work.

As for Mr. Gauguin, he was pretty much a perv.

One of his final homes in Tahiti was on property he tricked the Catholic mission to give him by claiming to be a good Christian. A total deception. Once he received the rights to the property, he stopped going to church. He built a two-story home there and named it "Maison Du Jouir" meaning *House of Orgasm* which, as you can imagine, did not sit well with the local priests.

The ungrateful bastard then filled the house with pornographic photos and he was constantly inviting the local teenage women to come and visit him. The locals could barely stand Paul and he smelled from a horrible syphilis infection.

As a final middle finger to the local parish who was so generous with him, he decided to name his dog "Penis." I'm not kidding. A moral contradiction of cinematic proportions, and yet he is also one of the most revered artists in history.

Meanwhile, back in France, Theo would gaze each day at the unwanted, rolled up canvases of Vincent and Paul. No one would buy them no less even look at them. It is estimated, at any given time, Theo would have in a small room at his gallery a display worth by today's standards over *One Billion Dollars* of Vincent and Paul's paintings … artwork that nobody considered at the time had any value.

"I shut my eyes in order to see."
Paul Gauguin

The 5-String Homestead

"Man is richest whose pleasures are cheapest."
Henry David Thoreau'

It was 1949 and he found a 17 acre plot on the side of a mountain near Beacon, New York, right off of a highway drifting along the Hudson River called 9D. Fifteen of the acres was essentially unusable, it was all slanted on the mountain but there was a nearly 2 acre flat ledge that was perfect for a home and it overlooked one of the widest sections of the Hudson river.

If she complained about it, she never did publicly. At least I'm not aware of it. But Pete Seeger somehow convinced his wife Toshi they should build their own log home on this plot of the mountain land. The property was purchased for about $100 an acre with money borrowed from family, Pete got an ax and started whacking away at the trees to collect enough timber to build what was essentially a one room homestead.

Now, Pete never built a log cabin before, there was no such thing as YouTube to learn how

others may have done it, there were no PBS stations airing shows like *"This Old House"* to give construction tips.

In one of the most envious displays of spousal support, Toshi not only agreed but she supported and helped and made the little cabin their home through one of the toughest economic times the family had to endure. Pete's career came to a crashing halt during the 1950s, just a few years after starting to build the cabin, when he was accused of being a communist and sentenced to one year in jail. Their income dried up to nothing.

Pete's friend and fellow Weavers member, Lee Hayes, would describe the dozens of hippies and admirers pitching tents on the property and lending a hand chopping trees, mixing concrete, hauling water and turning the dream into a home as *"Pete's Slave Labor Camps."*

Pete made sure a large window was placed overlooking the mighty Hudson River which later became a powerful part of his legacy because of the sloop Clearwater.

Through it all, Toshi helped and cheered everybody on. This was going to be the home, like it or not, of her children and her family. Pete had a dream, he was driven towards it, and she would make sure she supported whatever it was.

Because of that, Pete's log cabin and his time in Beacon, the influence of the Hudson river, the community of friends and musicians drawn to their home has become legendary. It was part of what made a living for them. More than just image, it became an envious way of life for many.

I found my own log cabin in Kentucky by happenstance, it just stumbled onto my life one day while driving through the country. I did not have to build mine from scratch but I viewed it as a home, a communal center of music and art, a place to bring up children… twins no less … who knew at the time I bought the cabin it would be their playground?

It's hard to merge home and music, Toshi had to tolerate Pete being gone sometimes for months at a time, tending her family in an unfinished log cabin with no running water and no indoor facilities. But she did it. And when Pete decided to build a boat and sail up the Hudson River and have shoreside concerts, Toshi was there organizing, raising money, raising children, raising gardens and organizing the dreams of her husband.

Toshi was an amazing cook, an amazing mother, an amazing gardener, she was an artist of Japanese heritage and a potter.

To focus on his work, letter writing and banjo playing, Pete built a small barn behind the Cabin with an upstairs room, a kind of an office, where he would spend his time home within walking distance of the family, typing letters and gluing tiny leaves to postcards before he would mail them.

I don't know if things like this can happen anymore. I don't know people are generous of spirit enough to support each other through intense life changes like that. We are by far a more selfish generation. But it occurs to me the more simple our lifestyle the more powerful our bonds can become.

I hope every Pete finds their Toshi, I hope every Toshi finds their Pete, I hope every family finds their rural palace, I hope each year brings kindness, loyalty, gentleness and peace to everybody.

Lord knows we need it.

And the sun came up, the sun went down.
The earth turned and the clock ticked.
And they are both gone.

"Whoever loves much can accomplish much,
for what is done in love is done well."
Vincent Van Gogh

The Elegance of Simplicity

Simplicity is best displayed in the details. Vincent's style offended the community of artists around him and most especially, the gallery owners. His brother found it virtually impossible to find patrons and art galleries interested in his brothers paintings. They were elementary, sloppy, and lacking the fine detail of the renaissance art style.

Here's a good example. *"Undergrowth with Two Figures"* was completed in 1890. As you get closer to the canvas you can see the wild, thick and rough strokes of his brush, the alternate layers of paint with thin strokes outlining the trees. Like a cartoon.

Raw, childish, beneath the dignity of the gallery owners and considered worthless by many, yet today this painting is valued at several million dollars.

When Vincent completed this canvas, he only had three months left to live.

"I'm such a nobody."
Vincent Van Gogh

Happy Little Trees

He was a retired military man working in a bar in Alaska, but all he wanted to do was paint. He and his wife had $1,000 in the bank and a young son. His wife was loyal and supportive, so together they decided he should journey off to seek his dream on the agreement that when the thousand dollars ran out, he would come home, be a good father and husband and do whatever it took to provide for his family.

He made his way to Florida to teach an art class attended by a woman who just lost her son. She didn't know who this teacher was but his calm and gentle demeanor made her depression ease. The woman and her husband convinced him to come to Virginia and to try art classes there, and he agreed.

Unfortunately, those classes failed and nobody would attend. He tried to do an evening class, but it was attended by only one man. Just one. The woman and her husband insisted they should cancel the class, but the artist said no, even just one student is a privilege.

At the end of that class that student said,

"I'm a businessman and I have a proposition. The fact that you would teach me, the single student, with such passion and dignity I have an offer: I will give you $1 million in exchange for 40% of everything you do for the rest of your life."

A million dollars to a broke artist. Wow. Yet he turned him down and continued his independent search for art in shopping malls and coffee houses. To save money in an age of consistent haircuts, he permed his hair so that he would not have to cut it so often.

He believed that doing what you love was more important than money, and doing what you love would eventually cause the money to come.

So, in 1982, he made his way to a small public television station in Northern Virginia. He would start his TV show with just a blank canvas and in exactly 30 minutes complete a painting. Each new painting was as a full television show.

The simplicity of the set, just a black curtain with an easel and two cameras in the studio, it was a very inexpensive program to produce. He made sure he wore a simple shirt because he felt shows about painting would last a long time, and he wanted to look just as current in 1992 as he did in 1982.

He developed a calm, serene style of speaking, describing it as talking to just one person, like a woman he loved while she was in bed. He was so easy to listen to because of the gentle nature of his unscripted dialogue. Sadly, the technical quality of the video and audio was so poor that after only one season the public television station dropped his show.

Another big problem he had when he started on TV was his hair was permed and he *hated* that hair. He *despised* his hair. He said he'd rather be bald but his hair became his trademark and it stayed with him the rest of his life.

Eventually he made his way to WIPB PBS in Muncie and started his TV series again with a better production quality.

He would complete an entire PBS season of 13 shows in a single week. He was very proud there was little to no editing, that he would complete every painting and every show within the 30 minutes that you see on television.

His method was very planned. He would complete a reference painting first as practice and then, when it was time to film, he would essentially be copying his reference painting. For season two, someone broke into his van and stole all 13 reference paintings so the entire season was filmed with ideas completely off the top of his head.

A man with a great sense of humor, everyone who worked with him insisted the person you saw on TV was exactly the same behind the scenes.

Constantly offering public and private appreciation to his wife Jane, he would always give her credit for allowing him the ability to pursue his dream. She constantly supported him and even worked behind the scenes to help manage the business side. Fiercely and passionately motivated, he even turned down an appearance on Oprah Winfrey because the segment did not allow him a chance to paint on the air.

Because he was on TV and famous the public assumption was that he was rich. The fact was there is little or no money to be made on public television, so he made a living teaching art classes, mostly in malls. This lasted until the latter part of his career when things really took off.

His greatest success was removing the fear of failure from those who wanted to try to paint.

When he died of cancer he was only 52 years old.

Even now, decades after he first began, the *Joy of Painting* and Bob Ross continues to be the most popular artist on public television.

"We don't make mistakes.
We just have happy accidents."
Bob Ross

Theo
Everybody needs a Somebody

Pete had his wife, Toshi. Henry David Thoreau had his mentor Ralph Waldo Emerson. Elvis had the Colonel and Dylan had Albert. For better or for worse, every Artist needs their champion, someone other than themselves who will fight to get their work seen and heard. It's no fun when you have to roll your own ball up the hill by yourself.

Vincent had his younger brother, Theo *(in Dutch you pronounce his name Tay-Yo)* and Theo, in turn, had his wife, Johanna.

Theo was an art dealer who promoted his brother's work relentlessly, but to no avail. That never stopped Theo from underwriting his brother's career allowing Vincent to completely devote himself to his painting. Their arrangement was simple: Theo paid Vincent to paint who, in return, would send Theo his completed work. In short, Theo owned all of Vincent's paintings.

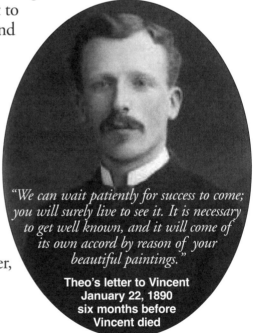

He died at the young age of 33, a very unpleasant death of paralysis and dementia brought on by the effects of syphilis. Theo's health declined rapidly after holding his brother on his deathbed just six months earlier, leaving Johanna alone with a young child and hundreds of unsellable paintings.

"We can wait patiently for success to come; you will surely live to see it. It is necessary to get well known, and it will come of its own accord by reason of your beautiful paintings."

Theo's letter to Vincent
January 22, 1890
six months before
Vincent died

About 10 years after Theo passed, Johanna struggled with all of these unmarketable canvases of her brother-in-law. She came from a family well connected in the art world. That was helpful to her, but dealers still had no use for any Van Gogh paintings. She finally found a Paris art dealer that was willing to show them and, like a lightning bolt out of the sky, Vincent became one of the most popular and in demand artists in the world.

Theo never got to see his brother's success, and Vincent died convinced he was a complete failure. If not for Johanna, the world may have never known the majesty of this great artist and the love and loyalty of his brother, her husband.

The
Dumbing Down
of the
Arts

We are living among the first generation in human history that is getting art as basic, 2-dimensional, flat screen digital reproductive images. Our senses and ears have been dumbed down to accept the crushed, brittle sound of an MP3 on tiny cell phone speakers versus the clarity of a stereo system.

Paintings and art have been reduced to a series of ones and zeros on tiny cell phone screens instead of an actual 3-dimensional canvas on a wall. We think we are not alone when we really are alone watching people online. Zoom concerts and live Facebook performances have become the new normal. We don't go to movie theaters, we stay on the couch and watch Netflix instead.

The dumbing down of art is part of the upheaval of our sense of humanity. The tsunami of digital cell phone music and imagery is killing performance spaces and galleries, even as the pandemic decimated over half of the music venues in America.

Part of the problem, and please don't take this wrong, is I'm seeing a lot of musicians and artists getting lazy. The only way to fight back this trend is to be *extremely* creative, really think things through before you engage in a project. Rattle the cage to the ground with your art, it's better to bust the cage than to be trapped in it. Don't just throw songs together, make your songs have an actual purpose, write something that's important. Don't just paint something because it's easy, paint something that is actually challenging. It does not have to be complicated, it just has to be unique.

Woody Guthrie was one of the most uncomplicated writers in music, his simple songs have stood the test of a century and his lyrics are still important. Vincent van Gogh was one of the most uncomplicated painters in history, and his canvases of elementary brushstrokes and basic forms have stood the test of time for generations. Their simplicity elevated the art form.

The dumbing down of the arts is crushing the essence of our culture. It is also an amazing and unique opportunity for all artists to simply be better.

One of the loudest warning signs about the decline of any culture is when art and music is removed from the education process of children. Don't get me started about what is happening in our schools. My heart goes out to these wonderful teachers who would love to be able to teach music and art but are being hamstrung by the bludgeoning of available budgets.

"Above all, we are coming to understand that the arts incarnate the creativity of a free people. When the creative impulse cannot flourish, then society severs the root of art."
John F. Kennedy

The
Contra-Factions
of
Van Gogh

*"Those who dream by day see many things
which escape those who dream only by night."*
Vincent van Gogh

Vincent wrote to his brother Theo daily. They have found over 900 letters to the brother who supported him all his adult life until he committed suicide, or was murdered, at 37 years old.

• Today he's the most valuable and famous artist in the world, but to his brother's great dismay he only sold one painting for a minimal amount during his lifetime.

• Vincent demanded Theo not discount the price of his paintings. It was an insult to him to reduce the price even if nobody was going to buy them.

• His painting career lasted less than 10 years.

• His baptism of color happened when he moved to Paris. It was in France that he unleashed the almost spiritual application of the oils on canvas.

**July Celebration in Paris
July 1886**

• His paintings today sell for tens of millions of dollars. And yet to other artists of his day he was amateur, childlike, and embarrassing. Here's an example. The famous church of one of his paintings ... the actual church, and then his finished canvas.

• His perspective often distorted, his color choices unrealistic, his brush strokes fat, rough and long, his paint, thick.

• His habit of outlining what he painted infuriated other artists to the point they refused to even be associated with him.

• He would often allow the bare canvas to show through his brushstrokes, using very stiff bristles, his brush almost scraping the canvas with paint.

• Before his brother arrived at his deathbed he wrote Theo a letter, stained with his own blood. Theo died only six months after Vincent passed away.

• Nobody remembers his critics. But they remember the artist and the loyal brother who believed and supported him.

• His common burial is an insult to the master he has become. Many of his paintings were stolen during the viewing.

The Story of
John Denver

He came up from absolutely nothing and complete failure, only to end up one of the biggest superstars worldwide in the 1970s. With over 100 million albums sold, he was rivaled only by Frank Sinatra, Elvis and the Beatles in chart success.

He grew up in a military family and when he decided he wanted to move to Los Angeles to pursue music, he had a heated disagreement with his parents. They wrote him a brutally harsh letter but included $200 to support their son.

He found a job for $100 a week as the opening act in a small club and made a good impression on the owner.

The owner brought him to Capitol records and, much to everybody's amazement, got the 20 year old kid a record deal. In the recording studio, nerves and inexperience overtook him, and for some strange reason he was unable to sing. Every song they recorded he was off key and when the record label heard the finished album, they dropped him immediately.

Just 20 years old, unable to sing properly, and dropped from a record label ... he was heartbroken and his dream of becoming a musician was shattered.

He joined a musical trio for a while, but the Beatles domination of American pop music obliterated their small careers so he left the group and went off on his own, singing in bars and coffee houses. Because he didn't have a record deal, he took every penny he had ... about $5000... and recorded his own self produced album.

He could only afford to press 250 copies and gave most of them away to friends and fellow musicians. One of the albums landed in the hands of another trio that was gaining momentum. On the album was a song called *"Babe I Hate To Go."* His friends, Peter Paul & Mary changed the name of the song to *"Leaving on a Jet Plane."*

That became the biggest song of their career, but the songwriter still struggled and was turned down by every record label in America. Finally an intern at a record company heard him singing and pushed his bosses to sign him. They reluctantly gave him an album deal.

And that's how RCA ended up with one of the biggest selling artists in American music history.

You would think that would make any musician happy, but to him it brought on the thunder clouds of darkness and depression. On the road constantly, mostly alone he turned to the trappings of the road. Performing to 20,000 people and then going back to a hotel room by himself was impossible.

Depression and the added guilt of what he was doing to his marriage created a perfect storm fueled by the growing abuse of alcohol. He was torn between two worlds: The alcohol-fueled life of being loved by thousands of people each night thinking you are virtually a God … and then the reality of coming home to a wife who despises your behavior and thinks you're a jerk.

John tried repeatedly to mend things with his wife, even writing one of the most passionate and beautiful love songs to her, called *Annie's Song* but his behavior and his increased alcohol abuse was too much and she demanded a divorce.

This so enraged the singer with the gentle, hippie and nature boy reputation, that he got a chainsaw and sliced his dining room table and marriage bed in half in an uncontrolled fury. Frightened and terrified, his wife began screaming. He lunged, grabbed her by the throat and began choking her. Realizing what he was doing, he stopped … but the marriage was forever finished.

Until the day of his death, when his small plane crashed into the ocean off the California coast, she remained the love of his life.

"The future of life on Earth depends on our ability to see the sacred where others see only the common."
John Denver

"I always think that the best way to know God is to love many things."
Vincent van Gogh

The Truth About
Making a Record

I see a lot of ads offering classes on recording an album, how to film or edit a music video. I see a tremendous amount of artists on social media talking about "their latest single" or the songs they are writing. It shows that Art is alive and well, the need for art and music is part of the human experience, and artists everywhere are trying very hard to find an audience.

It also shows the record industry, as we knew it, is dead.

I wrote a 9-minute song, described by reviewers as an epic *21st Century American Pie* (thank you Ken Cartwright, KYAC FM) all about the changes in music from Pete Seeger to Dylan to Hip Hop, and how all artists have a long, long way to go.

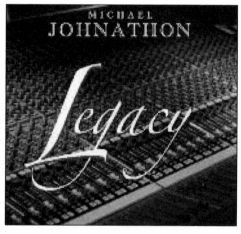

The truth is the music industry and the market, the ability to reach an audience, is so fractured, diluted and decimated that it is almost impossible for anybody to have what used to be called a "hit record." The very few artists getting signed anymore to what few record labels that remain often have massive investment packages behind them, secured from private investors.

That kind of financing is out of reach to most artists and so they are limited to what Facebook algorithms or email lists (often directed into Google trash files) can allow.

The only way an artist can sell their CDs, LPs and T-shirts is by performing in front of an audience… and the pandemic pretty much crushed that. Many have abandoned their dreams for secular jobs, and there's nothing wrong with that. There's no dishonor in that. But it is heartbreaking, even so.

The truth is the grand, epic albums of the past may be gone forever. Why? The financial transaction of music has been obliterated by streaming services, online free music, and the sheer exhaustion of musicians trying to make a living. There are no CD stores left in America except for the valiant, locally owned mom and pop stores, sadly far and few between.

Radio, even many public radio stations, have their playlists controlled by consultants, the new norm of the last 20 years. What you hear on a station in Peoria, for example, is decided upon by a consultant in Seattle, and so on.

A local artist with a new album is left out in the cold or the grace of a local DJ willing to roll the dice. There are not many WDHA FM *All Mixed Up* Jim Monaghan's left.

Once upon a time, you could get a half page feature in a hometown newspaper and see a bump in music sales or a surge on tickets for your show at a local club or festival. The problem is nobody reads newspapers and a half page story, even if you can get it because there are very few local writers at papers anymore, will be seen by very few readers. Getting a story posted on an online newspaper is almost useless ... unless you know the story is there ahead of time and where the URL is located. And that pretty much defeats the purpose of having the story posted.

My point is the ability to create financial transactions in the music industry is so limited the budgets are no longer there to create grand, cinematic albums like *Sgt Pepper, Pet Sounds, The Wall* and others. There's no way an artist can spend months in a recording studio creating a masterpiece.

The solution is for BMI, ASCAP and SESAC to eliminate venue licensing.
Convert to *Artist Licensing* instead, it will guarantee more employment, songwriters will get paid, and venues will open up

more music stages. It would be the same as a driver's license and will open up the ability for musicians to perform in front of audiences unencumbered by the threat of litigation. This is a practical solution, but that's a conversation for another chapter.

Artist licensing is the pathway for musicians to make a living again. The only way to sell your CDs and T-shirts is in front of a live audience ... and unless ASCAP, BMI and SESAC get out of the way it will remain difficult for most.

See my chapter about this in the book "WoodSongs 4" or visit MichaelJohnathon.com/BMI

It's a new normal. Artists need to do more than think out of the box, they need to crush the box and create a new one. In the end, no matter where you might think you are in your career, the aftermath of the current eruptions in the music industry means everybody has a long, long way to go.

Music *Should Be* Simple

"Watch the kids. Do like they do. Act like they act. Yell like they yell. Dance like they dance. Sing like they sing.

You'll be healthier. You'll feel wealthier. You'll talk wiser, you'll go higher, do better, and live longer.

I don't want the kids to be grownup, I want grown folks to be like kids."
Woody Guthrie

The Autograph

Unlike the other artists of his day, he did not sign his entire name to his paintings. Only his first name, *Vincent*. The reason, as he explained to his brother, he was tired of people not being able to pronounce "van Gogh."

To most folks, we pronounce it "van Go." In fact, for lack of a better phonetic spelling, it is pronounced "van Gok."

In July of 1890, his landlord noticed Vincent didn't come down for dinner. He found him in his room, lying in his bed drenched in a pool of blood. When he died a day later with his brother by his side, the local priest refused to give him a proper funeral because everyone assumed he committed suicide ... all because he would never say who actually shot him.

Days later, as Vincent was lowered into his eternal grave, Theo tossed sunflowers on top of his casket, the very flowers he loved so much to paint.

Today the most valuable paintings in the history of the art world were signed by a misunderstood, eternally sad and depressed, lonely artist who would only sign his first name, *Vincent*.

Both Sides Now

When you hate anyone or anything so deeply you can no longer see anything good in them, you are swimming in the stench of other people's opinions.

Nobody: left or right, man or woman, husband or wife, friend or foe, business partner, parent or child is intrinsically "evil." That debased status is reserved for those with no redeeming values. Unrepentant murderers, those harming children, etc.

Preferences are OK for any healthy relationship. It is valid to dislike someone, not approve of their political stance, to not participate in their religious beliefs or find comfort in their personality.

But to polarize your stance to the point of hating others simply because of their opinion ... that is part of the narcissistic epidemic sweeping cultures around the world.

I don't know anyone qualified enough to make that judgment about anybody. I'm seeing friends become former friends, family members blocking each other, acquaintances ridiculing the opinions of those they hardly know at all. It is all very sad and makes me worry about what the next few years will be like, especially for this generation of kids.

When opinions supersede reason, when it is strapped in disdain and hatred, when it ruptures communication and launches rage ... no good decision about anything can result.

I will sincerely try to never become so polarized in my point of view that I fail to see the good in a bad person, no matter how horrible their deeds.

That can be difficult, because sometimes the bad things a person does can overwhelm everything else about them.

But to deny there is anything good about someone equally denies our own imperfections. Hate is a poison, no matter how justified you might think that hate should be.

Let's face it: it is impossible to have a balanced exchange, acknowledging the good and bad, the right and wrong, the positives and negatives with someone who has become totally polarized in their thinking. Inability to acknowledge there are two sides to every issue is the epitome of closed mindedness, no matter which side you might be on. Narcissism is real, and it's a pain in the ass.

It's like convincing a brick wall to bend. The hardest state to achieve in human life is balance.

Just an opinion from a banjo playing Log Cabin dweller, not targeting anybody's stand about anything, just an overall viewpoint of what I see happening everywhere.

"The heart of man is very much like the sea, it has storms, tides and depths; it has its pearls too."
Vincent Van Gogh

"Darkness cannot drive out darkness; only light can do that. Hate cannot drive out hate; only love can do that."
Martin Luther King, Jr.

"Keep your face always toward the sunshine and shadows will fall behind you."
Walt Whitman

Vincent in Winter

He tried his best to fit into the artistic upper class of Paris, but his work and his personality was summarily dismissed. He complained to his brother in several letters how the anxiety of trying to fit in where he did not belong caused severe depression, so he started drinking a lot.

He was also tired of the cold and bitterness of winter, so he left Paris in mid-February 1888 for the warmer climate of sun-drenched southern Arles, France.

Unfortunately, the region was in the grips of a major cold spell and when he arrived and stepped off the train he was greeted by a snow storm. This was one of his first paintings finished after arriving. A small canvas, just 15 x 18" and painted in the style of the many Japanese prints he so admired, this is one of the few winter scenes Vincent portrayed in oils.

He had but one more winter left to live.

Tiny Brush Strokes

One of my favorite Van Gogh paintings is this one, especially for the absolute detail of the tiny brushstrokes.

"Road with Cypress and Star" was the last canvas completed during his stay in Saint-Rémy-de-Provence, France.

The previous summer, in June 1889 he painted his famous *The Starry Night,* an imaginative scene from the window of his room at the asylum. Aside from the swirling energy of the stars, a dominant figure in that canvas was the cypress tree. A little known item of history about *The Starry Night* is that he offered it to fellow painters Emile Bernard and Paul Gauguin as a gift ... and both turned it down.

Now, almost a year later he is becoming more comfortable with his infatuation with the shape of the cypress trees. This painting accelerates the brushstrokes style of *The Starry Night* into something truly amazing. He wrote to Theo about this painting:

"I still have a cypress with a star from down there, a last attempt - a night sky with a moon without radiance, the slender crescent barely emerging from the opaque..."

While writing this letter, he did not realize it truly was his last attempt, he had less than two months left to live.

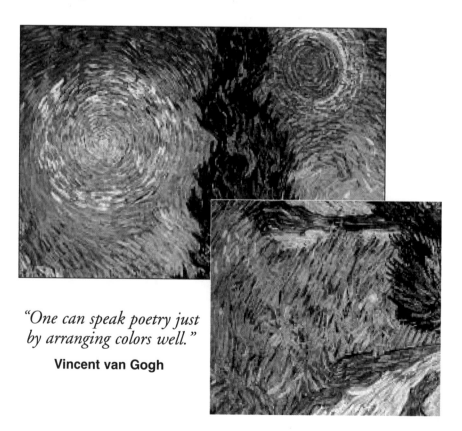

"One can speak poetry just by arranging colors well."
Vincent van Gogh

The Scream

For as long as I can remember I have suffered from a deep feeling of anxiety which I have tried to express in my art."
Edvard Munch

Influenced by neo impressionism, he grew up surrounded by depression, poverty, severe illness and outright insanity. At five years old his mother died of tuberculosis, followed by the death of his beloved sister. His father fell into a deep depression, often intently praying for days on end.

In 1885, still in his 20s, he journeyed to Paris to experience the world of art. While there he was exposed to impressionists, other artists and was heavily influenced by the styles of Monet, Renoir, Gaughan and van Gogh.

He adapted the impressionist brushstroke but never fully embraced the impressionist style. He interpreted his feelings of emotional emptiness by using bold strokes and bright colors, a contradiction of his internal confusion.

His early efforts as an artist were a dismal and total failure. By middle-age he suffered a complete nervous break down and severe, acute alcoholism.

Turning back to Art for comfort, he literally triumphed over his dark history. He decided to work out his feelings of loss and sadness, his psychological turmoil, on canvas with oils. He used his melancholy to create a series of over 100 finished canvases and presented his very first gallery showing.

In a letter to a friend he described how darkness, sickness and death were the "black angels" that inspired his artistic success.

About 53 of his paintings were shown in Berlin but the exhibition was an embarrassing failure and closed in less than a week. Critics called his work an *"insult to Art."* The public completely rejected him, however the gossip and furor actually made him somewhat famous.

By 1893, he finished an unusually intense painting, an vivid portrayal of sheer emotional terror and turmoil, a painting that reflected the volcano of fear and sadness in his own soul. Walking alone one evening during a summer visit to Norway, overwhelmed by loneliness and isolation, he watched a blood red sun setting in the distance and felt inside his heart a powerful and undeniable bellowing, a shriek of shear agony and horror.

Edvard Munch took this intense emotion and applied it to canvas, a painting called *"The Scream"* which became a definitive artistic statement of the 20th century.

The actual title is *Der Schrei der Natur (The Scream of Nature)*, and the Norwegian title is *Skrik (Shriek)*.

By the turn of the century, his depression and alcoholism began to overtake his very existence. He was a mess. A relationship with a woman caused great turmoil, as one day she threatened suicide with a gun and, as he grabbed her to take the gun away, she shot one of his fingers. By 1908 he got into an argument with another artist and attempted to kill him with a gun.

While in Copenhagen he suffered another breakdown and spent eight months in a mental hospital.

Unlike van Gogh and others, Edvard decided to overcome his illness and, remarkably, made a complete and full recovery. Unfortunately, his sobriety affected his artistic output. His post breakdown images were described as "beige in emotion," referred to as placid and uninteresting. Of course, that beige is now worth millions.

He lived for another three decades and died in 1944.

*"From my rotting body flowers shall grow
and I am in them and that is eternity."*
Edvard Munch

As the
Frost Descends

This has been such a hard time for so many. And I don't imply anything political here, just a musician's observation.

There is a frustration and anger in the air that many watch with caution and alarm. The *Me First* generation learned to accept narcissism as norm, as advertisers sold America on everything they "deserved" to buy.

We are a generation drowning in global debt, ill prepared for love, empathy and patience. Society exists on a massive credit card, millions are out of work and hundreds of thousands are standing in food lines. This is not the world the "me first" generation knows how to deal with, this is not a world those sold on "everything they deserve to buy" know how to handle.

This is where contentment, music and art, gentleness and patience become the most valuable commodity we can possess. Kindness and love, two words that became Kumbaya catchphrases have now become the most powerful forms of transaction.

There is a frost falling across the world as a mental Covid-19 keeps its grip on us, as social media streams become inundated with those who have succumbed to an emotional virus that has riddled society with confusion.

Love and kindness is the warmth that will chase the frost away ... if we let it. Patience and understanding will fuel the fires as they provide escape from the coldness of what is happening.

If we let it.

I hope, during the dark months of winter, as the economy, frustration, vitriol, politics, negative news and a rampant virus seem to inundate everyone in a tsunami of stress, we remember the power of contentment, your front porch and the music of your living room couch.

As frost falls across the land we do well to remember the lessons and lifestyles of our rural generations that came before us, those who learned to be rich with just a little, to achieve the treasure of contentment, the compassion of community, the art form of sharing and the welcoming spirit of love and kindness.

To me, that is the spirit of the Front Porch. That is the theme of everything I do, artistically and musically. It is family and friends, banjos and fiddles, neighbors and Main Street hardware stores, cookies and home made bread, holding hands and good morning kisses.

"Some are excited by the smell of gun powder, but how much saner to be excited by the smell of new bread."
Henry David Thoreau

The Shortest Story

He didn't have the "best" voice, but he had the most energy. He only had 4 songs enter the top 40, performed 2,000 concerts in 10 years and raised over $6 million for over 100 charities.

He wasn't exactly a big hit maker, his signature song *"Taxi"* only went to number 24 on the Billboard singles chart. But what a trailblazer. He ended up writing and performing some of the longest story songs in popular music.

As a youngster he struggled with severe asthma, so singing wasn't exactly on his radar.

Before his music career took off he had a love of film-making, and a documentary that he wrote and directed about boxing was nominated for an Academy award. He worked on over 300 films before turning exclusively to music.

A musical van Gogh, Harry rarely got good reviews for his recordings and songs, but his fan base was huge and loyal. So much for critics.

His wife, Sandy, wrote a poem about her first husband's strained relationship with his father. One day she showed it to Harry, who did not think much of it at the time. About a year and a half later, she brought the poem out again as his career kept him away from home ... and this time the poem resonated deeply.

He took the poem, reworked it and made it rhyme, turned it into a song that became the number one single in the nation ... which kept him away from home even more.

On the afternoon of July 16 Harry drove to a meeting in Manhattan with his agents, the purpose was to convince Harry to slow his schedule down and focus more on his family and career. While on the Long Island Expressway his car lost power and a truck plowed into the little Volkswagen and we lost Harry.

That night he was supposed to do a benefit concert in Long Island. Nearly 30,000 fans waited at the park for Harry to start his concert when a voice came over the announcement system saying that he was gone.

He was only 38 years old.

His manager, Ken Kragen used Harry's efforts to end Word Hunger to help organize the massive charity song, *"We are the World."* A documentary on Harry has been released, *"When in Doubt, Do Something."* He was an inspirational artist.

Donate if you can:
HarryChapinFoundation.org

And if you want to hear something that will rattle your soul, look up his song *"Shortest Story"* it will be the most moving two minutes of your musical life.

His family, led by his Grammy winning brother Tom, continues his legacy of good work. It is something we should all aspire to, right? In honor of Harry I am including that song he wrote after reading the poem written by his wife, *Cats in the Cradle* on the enclosed album, *The Painter.*

"Our lives are to be used and to be lived as fully as possible, and it seems that we are never so alive as when we concern ourselves with other people."
Harry Chapin

Autumn

"As long as autumn lasts, I shall not have hands, canvas and colors enough to paint the beautiful things I see."
Vincent Van Gogh

Alright, I will admit it, I'm a sucker for anything autumn.

Here is a fascinating study of the Van Gogh "contradiction." His sense of perspective and light frustrated, even angered fellow artists and patrons.

Notice the direction of light is wrong: the shadows cast by the trees don't match those cast by the lady.

Called *"Avenue of Poplars in Autumn"* finished in October, 1884 not long after Thoreau roamed Walden woods across the Atlantic.

Vincent wrote to his brother Theo, he felt this wasn't something he considered very sellable, not even Vincent liked it.

Today this "unprofessional" effort is worth millions at auction.

Sunset for Sparky

"Be yourself. No one can say you're doing it wrong."
Charles M. Schulz

As a kid I was a huge fan of Charles Schulz and his *Peanuts* cartoon strip, I even created my own cartoon strip published in 17 newspapers. For a time, cartooning was going to be my future not music. I was only 16 years old.

His nickname was Sparky. Since he was six he knew he wanted to be a cartoonist. He created the *Peanuts* ... Charlie Brown, Lucy, Linus, Snoopy and crew ... at a time when newspapers were healthy and strong, starting out with only seven papers but ended up being the most successful cartoon strip in history.

Like many artists, even Vincent, Charles struggled with depression. By the 1970s, with over 300 million daily readers, he was earning $1 million every month. The demise of the American newspaper saw the virtual elimination of this wonderful art form. These days the cartoon strip has been replaced by single panel, digital memes.

I painted *"Sunset for Sparky (Tribute to Peanuts)"* 18x24 oil on canvas. A rather strange idea ... how simple can a painting be and stay interesting?

"I am not afraid of storms,
for I am learning how to sail my ship."
Louisa May Alcott

The
Final Summer
of
The Painter

Vincent spent the last two months of his life at the Ravoux Inn in France during the summer of 1890. Given to an absolute schedule, he would get up every morning about 5 AM and paint all day, coming back to the Inn at his regular time each evening for his dinner at the downstairs café. He would then go up to his room and paint some more.

He was charged about 3 francs a night and befriended the owners 13 year old daughter. After unrelenting requests, he finally painted the young girl and gave her the canvas as a gift.

During that summer he created more than 80 paintings before the shooting. Here is the Ravoux inn Auvers-sur-Oise where Vincent stayed and a photo of his room:

Mistakes ❧ Masterpieces

We live in a world desperate for kindness, understanding, love and forgiveness. It is safe to say most mistakes that occur in our lives are unintended. Sometimes we are even mistaken about mistakes. Heck, didn't Vincent feel *The Starry Night* was a big flop and total failure? That was a mistake, indeed.

Mistakes happen. They will always happen, it's part of our imperfect existence. How much better it is to view our mutual imperfections with the same kindness towards others as we hope they will return back to us.

Treated with a sense of humor and a forgiving spirit, mistakes can become part of the humorous dialogue of life as we move on to the next mistake. Patience becomes important.

And, sometimes, those mistakes can become masterpieces.

"Keep room in your heart for the unimaginable."
Mary Oliver

Newspapers

I love good, well written hometown newspapers. America was built on rustling pages turning on a Sunday morning or over coffee in a cafe somewhere. We need them. But folks don't buy papers anymore, they read the news on cell phones. A harsh fact.

Four times this morning I tried to read an online news story, and four times I was blocked from reading it unless I subscribed to the newspaper. This is such a backwards business model and I do not understand why papers, already struggling, guarantee failure by insisting on pushing this foolishness.

Radio and TV are also ad-based business models. When a radio station posts an article, you get to see it. When you see it you also see all the ads businesses paid for in the hopes that you will see their advertising. This is no different for newspapers except the papers insist that you get blocked from seeing the advertising unless you pay a subscription.

This is not only a disservice to the audience but it is a huge disservice to the advertiser, and I cannot imagine investing on a platform designed to prevent an audience from seeing my ad, no less the content that is supposed to attract that very audience.

The more eyes on your website, the more value to the advertiser ... and the more likely businesses will place ads on your website. A newspaper website costs no more and no less than any radio or TV station's website and they all allow free access.

It is not brain surgery. I wish newspapers would see the value of *attracting* an audience, not preventing them from accessing the content. Lower your newsstand price, increase the size of your font, and focus on local news and arts, not wire stories that people got yesterday on their cell phones.

We need good journalists, and access to thorough, accurate information. We need good newspapers. And comics.

The Saint-Paul Asylum

This is a rare painting, not one of his more famous works, of what it looked like outside of his window at the Saint Paul asylum in France. Vincent checked himself into the facility voluntarily as he struggled, descending deeper into his depression and mental illness, no doubt fueled by his perceived failure as an artist.

Can you imagine what it felt like to pour himself into his work and to be told over and over again it wasn't good enough? They said it looked sloppy, it wasn't professional, the public won't buy it, the gallery owners wouldn't show it.

Theo tried so hard, only to have a single painting sold in Vincent's lifetime.

Even in despair, Vincent still saw the world in bright, bold and cheerful colors with brushstrokes demanding attention. Yet in his heart, he felt the volcanic tremors of failure. It must've been very hard when he wrote to Theo:

"I will never amount to anything as an artist, I just know it."

Think of that next time you try something and you are ridiculed or degraded, especially by someone close to you. When criticism comes from those you love, it can wrench your soul from your chest. It can be a deep wound.

Be like Vincent, we must all carry-on with boldness, driven by love for your work, not for the desire of success … for in the end that is the true and only path to success.

$imply Million$

Here is a close-up of one of Vincent van Gogh's self portraits, worth nothing when he painted it but now valued in the millions of dollars.

Notice the bold style of his brushstrokes, long and full of paint, very unlike the near perfection of many of the artists of his day. Their work was almost photographic, they were so perfect.

By contrast, van Gogh was almost childlike in his approach to painting. His habit of outlining his subjects would drive other artists and gallery owners crazy. So amateur, so sloppy, so without technique.

When you look at his paintings you are faced with the painful realization that, frankly, he really was not all that "good."

So what changed? When he died at the end of the century he was a broken, penniless, sick and ignored artist who couldn't sell a thing. Ten years later, his reputation was exploding worldwide and his status as a legend was taking off.

So, again, what changed? Look at the almost careless way he paints. It is the handiwork of a great craftsman who did not complicate his art. His paintings did not change. His style did not change. His "amateur" approach to his canvases did not change. His sloppy, long brushstrokes did not change. His thick use of layers upon layers of paint did not change.

What changed was other peoples opinion. What created value to van Gogh was not just the quality of his art, it was the opinion of the market place that added that value. Van Gogh remains a not very good "technical" painter by critical standards, but his canvases are worth millions because public opinion changed.

Clearly, Vincent's artwork is absolutely brilliant. What I think makes it so is, unlike the other artists of his era who aspired to near photographic perfection of the brushstrokes, his artwork seemed accessible. His artwork made the audience feel like, well, they could do it, too.

Van Gogh was to the art world what Bob Dylan and Woody Guthrie are to the music world. Their songs are simple, with rudimentary, predictable chord patterns and standard tuning. What makes their music so attractive is their accessibility. Folks want to play them because they can. They are so simple they are considered a genius.

That is why van Gogh's paintings are worth millions. That is why they are reproduced, copied and studied. His paintings are so simple they are complicated, so simple they are genius.

"Anybody can be complicated,
it takes a genius to be simple."
Woody Guthrie

Hot Dogs & Pete Seeger

It is believed the very first American hot dog – once called *'dachshund sausages'* – was sold by a German immigrant out of a food cart in New York City in the 1860s. Ten years later, another German, Charles Feltman, opened the first hot dog stand on Coney Island. He sold over 3,600 *"frankfurters"* that year.

This is a TRUE STORY:

My very first job after I got my driver's license was on a tiny four-cylinder blue Subaru flatbed Hot Dog truck with a collapsible umbrella and boilers in the back selling hotdogs in my hometown of Beacon, New York.

On the door of the little powder blue truck, in bold white letters, it said *"Joe's Hot Dogs."* Of course everybody thought my name was Joe and I spent more time explaining that it was the name of the guy who owned the truck then I did actually selling the long, snappy Sabrett hotdogs with mustard and onion relish.

It was not an easy job, not so much because it was hard work, but I simply did not like hotdogs and the constant smell of them was not exactly a good working environment for me.

I would often park in front of the Grand Union grocery store along Main Street. One very warm day when business was slow I walked into the grocery store to cool off in its air condition-ing. I would walk the isles so as not to seem like I was loitering. When I came to the vegetable section, there loading up his cart with a massive amount of strawberries was Pete Seeger.

He was buying up as many strawberries as he could find because his Clearwater festival along the local Hudson River bank had sold out of his famous strawberry shortcake. I recognized him because I saw him perform one day when I was in high school. I introduced myself, said hello, telling him I was a wanna-be musi-cian. He was very friendly and he invited me to the festival that weekend. Tickets were free, a good price for an unsuccessful teenage hot dog vendor.

I showed up, and Pete recognize me from across the field and waved for me to come over and introduced me to his wife, Toshi. Another young boy, I recall he was from Pawling, walked up and interrupted us because he wanted to show Pete his concert poster with his own name in huge letters.

By now there was a crowd of a dozen or so that were waiting to visit with Pete, but he saw the young teenage boy and his grandiose poster, took the poster and put his hand on the boys shoulder and directed him to a tree where they both sat down on the grass and Pete explained why his name needed to be smaller.

Years later, it deeply impressed me that someone as famous is Pete Seeger would ignore his gathering fans to help counsel a young kid that he did not even know.

I struck up a friendship with Pete and Toshi after that, well, as much of a friendship is you could have with Pete. But they were always kind, I could call them up and they would let me stop by their mountainside cabin and I was always careful to keep my visit brief. As they did with so many others.

The next year, Toshi called me up and invited me to come perform a set on the stage of the Clearwater Strawberry Festival. I was a nervous wreck, but there I was on stage singing in front of what seemed like a million people to me at the time. All of a sudden, as I was singing an old Uncle Dave Macon song, I heard someone humming in the speaker. I turned to my right, and there Pete had walked out on stage to hum the harmony to this old traditional song with me.

Good Lord, I was on stage performing with Pete Seeger. I don't remember much after that, I assume I finished the song and everything went OK.

A pretty amazing experience for a young boy with dreams of becoming a musician made possible by a sworn vegetarian and hot dogs that I don't even like.

"It's been my belief that learning how to do something in your hometown is the most important thing."
Pete Seeger

Henri Matisse

At 19 years old he started his painting career as a traditional artist. His first finished canvas was of library books on a table. Dark, realistic, detailed. Boring.

So on he painted. He was pursuing his painting career for over 15 years, he was now in his mid-30s with three children, and Henri Matisse was flat broke.

On a journey to France he rediscovered the colorful dyes in the factories around his boyhood home and decided to overhaul and simplify his view of art. Drastically simple.

Critics hated his work, calling him the "bad boy" of impressionism. Gallery owners considered him an absolute lunatic. Thanks to a Russian millionaire who purchased his paintings in bulk, he became one of the wealthiest European artists.

Referring to the Russian's adoration of Matisse, one writer complained: *one lunatic paints them, the other buys them.*

Look at the details in darkness of his first painting, and then look at his most famous canvas of all: *the Blue Nude.* Singular in color, drastically simple in lines and yet this painting has traveled the world.

Pastor van Gogh

In his early years, Vincent pondered becoming a minister and for a while trained at the seminary. His religious paintings are not well known, here is an example of *La Résurrection de Lazare* his effort to copy the godly style of Rembrandt.

"The Starry Night" painted in June 1889, shows the view from the window of his asylum room at Saint-Rémy-de-Provence, just before sunrise. For the canvas, he added an imaginary steeple. It is considered by many an interpretation of his religious views, the worship of a creator in the shadow of a church. To many the work represents Vincent's struggle with his belief in God and his disappointment in the church.

In any case, it is one of the most recognizable, reproduced and valuable canvases in history. Vincent tried to offer the painting as a gift to other artists, but they didn't like it and it was refused.

Horny Vincent
and the
Pink Peach Trees
Souvenir de Mauve

Here is a little known, rarely seen canvas. Completed in 1888, a year before his passing, unusual in that the painting is both signed and titled.

The art teacher Anton Mauve was a cousin of Vincent. When van Gogh attended The Hague, his cousin was willing to teach him the use of oil paint and watercolour. Sadly, the relationship between the two painters did not last very long.

When van Gogh started sleeping with an unmarried mother and prostitute, Mauve, was horrified and he broke off all contact with Vincent.

Still, van Gogh always fondly remembered the painter. When Mauve died, Vincent signed this painting with *"Souvenir de Mauve"* and sent it as a gift to the artist's widow.

The Ear Thing

The story about van Gogh cutting off his ear has new enlightenment due to some recent document discoveries.

The fable is the evening before Christmas Eve 1888 Vincent had an argument with Paul Gauguin, followed him in the dark with a knife and when Paul saw him creeping from behind Vincent ran back to his apartment in a fit of rage and cut off his own *lower ear lobe*. He wrapped it in a cloth and went to a brothel and gave it to a prostitute name Rachel, who then reportedly fainted.

The truth has been clarified by a recently discovered document, now on display at the van Gogh Museum in Amsterdam. It was written by the doctor who treated van Gogh, Dr. Felix Rey, who Vincent didn't exactly like very much.

It seems Vincent cut off his *entire* ear except for the lower ear lobe. He did wrap it in a cloth, went to the brothel but gave it to a 19-year-old chambermaid, not a prostitute, named Gabriella. Her face was disfigured from an attack by a dog many years earlier and it seems Vincent was offering a delusional kindness with his gift of the cut off ear.

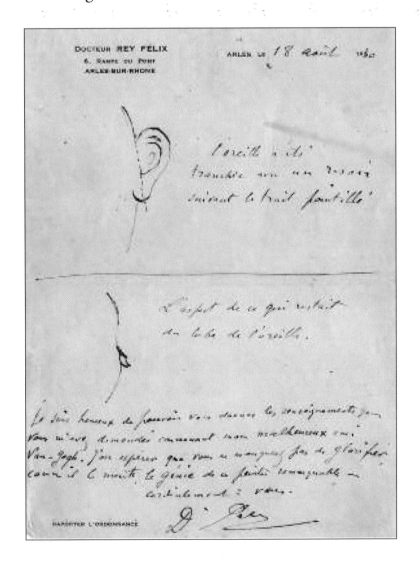

Picasso

Young 25-year-old Pablo Picasso, from Spain, grew up around his father who liked to paint portraits of pigeons. This inspired him to take up his own artwork. At 25 years old he decided to journey to Paris to try his life as an artist.

He was completely penniless, almost living on the street when he finished this painting of nude women that launched the movement of modern Art, a style called cubism and Pablo turned Paris upside down.

His career mingled with the final days of van Gogh and the work of Monet but he pursued his own unique vision.

He was barely 15 when he created his first major work, stunning the art community of Barcelona. It was a painting subject he and his father chose together, a young woman's first communion. It showed young Pablo was fully capable of following the footsteps of major artists like Rembrandt and Michelangelo.

But he chose a different path. He turned away from the artwork of his father and his teachers. He "unlearned" it. He fell into the company of morally questionable people and began frequenting the bars and brothels of Barcelona. This so infuriated his father that he cut young Pablo off from his allowance and turned him away, to face the future on his own.

Picasso soon fell in love with a young woman named

Germaine. Unbeknownst to him, his best friend also fell in love with her. While Picasso was out of town, his friend called a dinner that included Germaine, announced his great passion for her, bemoaned her rejection of him, pulled out a revolver and shot himself in the head right there in the café. Picasso was so shaken he painted a private canvas of his friend on

his deathbed, keeping this painting hidden for half a century and only revealed its existence 50 years later.

But he was just 25 years old, not a penny in his pocket and alone when he began his journey in Paris. At 25 years old, the rebellious young man rejected his father's last name and took on his mother's maiden name and from then on sign his paintings only as Picasso. At 25 years old, he had the singular dream to become the greatest artist that ever lived. His new artwork confounded the public and critics, most thought his work was elemen-

tary and juvenile ... but sold for millions of dollars, making him one of the most successful artists of the 20th century.

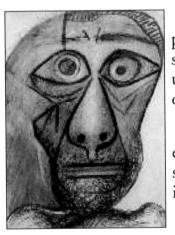

He stayed in his studio all the time, painting at night in silence and did not socialize. He rarely used brushes, did not use an easel and preferred to paint on top of newspapers spread out on the floor.

He passed away in 1973. One year earlier he was looking in the mirror and saw his own death. One of his final paintings was the image he saw in that mirror.

Painters ❧ Women

*"When a woman gives herself to a man, he owns all women.
When she refuses him, he pursues all women."*

Artists tend to be an emotional bunch. This is a comment attributed to Rembrandt who, like Van Gogh and Mozart, died in complete obscurity, drowning in failure, owning nothing, always in love and always alone. Many would frequent brothels because it was hard to maintain relationships ... most ended up with syphilis.

He was once the most admired painter in Europe. He specialized in portraits of the wealthy to make money. Later, he fell from grace, living across from an amusement park with drunks on his front step. His style was brilliant detail, layering his paint often with a knife.

A borderline con man, he often bid against his own work to drive up the prices. He was a shopaholic and eventually lost his fortune and couldn't pay his bills. The Dutch artist community even banned him from selling his own paintings. One of his last commissions, considered his masterpiece, was rejected so he cut up the canvas in pieces.

Ready for this? The great artist Rembrandt Harmenszoon van Rijn died a pauper, bankrupt and a has-been, alone and was buried in an unmarked grave.

In the 20th century many of his collected works were discovered to be forgeries at a loss of millions to collectors.

It's the Little Things

You may not be a famous musician filling arenas around the world, but you love music and invite your friends to your front porch. *It makes your friends happy.*

You may not be a famous cook like Martha Stewart, producing grand meals on national television, but you make healthy dishes for your family. *It makes your family happy.*

You may not be a university educated environmentalist carrying picket signs in front of nuclear power plants or protesting strip mining around the country, but you keep your home and your property clean. *It makes your earth happy.*

You may not be a corporate farmer owning thousands of acres providing national food chains with grain and crops, but you have a small organic garden growing enough tomatoes to share with your friends. *It makes your neighbors happy.*

You may not be Rembrandt creating magnificent works of art, but you love doing small paintings and art projects that you share as gifts with people you care about. *It lets them know that you love them.*

You may not be a world famous actress or look like a centerfold model, but you respect your husband and take care of your family and try your best to be a good partner. *It makes your husband happy.*

You may not be an incredibly handsome weight lifter or a rich man making millions, but you love your wife and you buy her small gifts and bring her flowers to let her know how much you care about her. *It makes your wife happy.*

You may not be a highly paid architect creating skyscrapers across the horizon of major cities, but you've built your children a little playground with your own two hands. *It makes your children happy.*

You may not be a high-powered attorney, but you can defend yourself, your reputation and your dignity without a word. *And that will make your conscience satisfied.*

You may not have accomplished big things in this small life, but all your little things can add up to a big life. And it can make *you* happy.

Never underestimate your ability to contribute, create, participate and offer others around you. Things don't have to be big to be important.

Your "little" self matters.

"Normally I'm against big things. I think the world is going to be saved by millions of small things."
Pete Seeger

photo by Harold Dunsmore

Be Inspired
but you must
Never Copy

I was visiting Pete's cabin in Beacon, New York one evening and there was another songwriter there trying very hard to sound like the next Bob Dylan. As the evening ended and we were getting ready to leave, Pete walked with me out to my car and asked if I noticed anything odd tonight. I joked and said it was really nice having Dylan in your living room, and he put his hand on my shoulder and said the above words.

"Be inspired but you must never copy."

I think there are a lot of artists right now influenced by Pete and wanting very much to honor him with a tribute of some kind. All that is fine. I see many others trying to create their own audience by siphoning off of his and I don't I think Pete would have wanted that. I know for sure Toshi wouldn't.

There's a lot of good projects out there, Rik Palieri and Richard James Nestler have an album of rare maritime songs Pete used to sing. John McCutcheon has a fine tribute album as well. But there are too many others trying to become Seeger clones. Pete had a great eye for originality and was very generous with his support. He was *inspired* by Woody, but he never tried to sound, act or *copy* himself as the next Woody Guthrie.

I learned something important at his cabin that night and I was determined to find a unique path fueled by the inspiration artists like Pete, Woody, Dylan and so many others gave me. I don't know that I've succeeded, but I'm trying. It's a very hard road out there and we don't have the benefit of a healthy music and media industry that Pete had during his prime.

I do know one thing, my failure will be uniquely my own.

The Kid *with the* Wrists

In 1953, a lonely, skinny boy came off the train and signed up to be part of the Negro baseball leagues. He was just a kid with no idea of the historic storm he was walking into.

All he wanted to do was play ball, but the crowds were small and the money was almost nonexistent. He never gave up and he eventually got signed to a major league team in Atlanta.

He was just a kid, a black kid playing baseball in the deep South on a white baseball team in a town dominated by the white culture. But the power in his wrists proved to be stronger than the prejudice that surrounded him.

He was just a kid. But one by one, game by game, swing by swing his towering home runs proved to be stronger than the hate he faced.

Every at bat, the superhuman strength of his black wrists whipped the wooden bat around, slamming into the ball and send it towering into the outfield bleachers across America as his home run tally began to mount.

Then home run 699 happened and it seemed like the whole planet suddenly realized the skinny black kid from the deep south was about to overtake the most precious record in all of baseball: Babe Ruth's unbeatable record of 714 home runs.

To many this was sacrilegious. This could *not* happen. This was *not* allowed. A black man, of all things, should *not* be permitted to become the king of America's favorite pastime over an icon like Babe Ruth.

He was still just a kid ... and day by day, letter by letter, telegram by telegram the death threats mounted and became more alarming, more violent ... more real.

Security was hired, police lined the baselines and the TV announcers commented on the danger every time he came to bat, making the risk even more dramatic.

And then one day, after he tied the magic number of 714, it happened.

The skinny black kid who got off the train in 1953 stood in the batter's box, his powerful wrists crushed into the ball pitched by another black man, Al Downing, hurling at nearly 100 miles an hour toward him. He swung ... and the whole world watched as the ball sailed high up to the heavens and into the outfield bleachers.

As he ran his victory lap around the bases, he had no idea if a bullet would come out of the stands somewhere, if a high-powered rifle was being aimed at his head as he rounded second base. But he made it home.

That skinny black kid who walked off the train so long ago touched home base with his feet as the reigning homerun king of the world in baseball.

"When you hear all your life you're not good enough, it makes you wonder if the other guys have something you've never seen before. If they do, I'm still looking for it."
Hank Aaron

Today's
Scrambled Eggs
can be tomorrow's
Deposit Slip

Songs can come at the most awkward, annoying moments. And they can come in rushes... the cool guitar lick that you really like, the melody inside a chord pattern that is new to you, rolling around in your heart and your spirit for days and days and then another one comes along and it does the same thing and before you know it you have a bottleneck of guitar pieces and chords and melodys... and not a single lyric. Nada.

And it usually happens while you were overwhelmed with other responsibilities, projects or activities and you don't have time to let your heart and spirit speak in poetry because you are inundated with everything else.

But the guitar licks are fun and the melody is solid and it really is a song ... it's just simply devoid of the message. So you wait. And you make up fake lyrics to fill the lines to test the melody of the song knowing full well those will never, never become the words.

A long, long time ago Paul McCartney woke up with a melody in his head. He had no words and he would hum the tune to others to see if they had ever heard it before. And he kept repeating the lyric *"scrambled eggs"* over and over again because it fit the melody line but he knew that would never become the actual words to the song.

And then one day his spirit relaxed, his heart opened in silence away from John, The Beatles, business and everything else the words flowed and the poetry fit the melody just perfectly. And that melody with the odd *"scrambled eggs"* lyric became the most recorded pop song in the history of modern music:

He called it *Yesterday*

Don't misunderstand, I'm not implying anything I write now, in the past or in the future will ever be as spectacular as what scrambled eggs became. I'm simply describing the process of the bottleneck of music against the dark void of the lyric. Sometimes you have to wait. Patience. The gates will eventually open and you have to be ready.

"I don't work at being ordinary."
Paul McCartney

They Persisted

They did not like his choices, who his friends were or who he chose to sing to ... which was *everybody*. America was angry with Pete Seeger. His career collapsed, his income dried up and he and his wife had to make a decision: get a real job or continue as musician.

They looked failure in the face and decided being a musician wasn't just his job, it is what he was, what he was best at, and what he loved. He felt he could do the most good singing to audiences.

His wife, Toshi, could easily have condemned this and made it impossible for Pete to continue. She lived in a half built log cabin on the side of a mountain along the Hudson river with very few middle-class conveniences. Pete was gone a great deal and she was left home alone for months at a time, tending the property, growing the garden, and taking care of their young children.

Meanwhile, Pete was out with his guitar and banjo performing for $25 or $50 at a time at schools, children's camps, every once in a while a college. He was performing to kids all over the country while his own kids stayed at home without their dad.

Times were hard. He was humiliated. He was not liked. He was misunderstood and ridiculed. They made fun of him and called him names. And he lost almost everything ... except Toshi.

But he persisted. And so did she. Together.

It was a risky decision. Nobody knows what tomorrow brings, nobody knows for sure the results of their choices. All you can do is have a goal, a vision ... a dream ... and hope it turns out for the best. I can't imagine what the conversations were like in the evening, in the quiet, in the dark, alone as a couple. After Toshi passed, Pete often wished he spent more time with her, paying attention to what *she* wanted.

Dreams are born of hard work and watered by the absolute determination to never quit.

The Story of York

In 1804, President Thomas Jefferson asked Meriwether Lewis & William Clark to hike across the continent and find a trail that led to the Pacific Ocean. Clark's childhood slave, a black man named York, traveled with them as a valuable part of the expedition team.

Lewis wrote in his journal about the day York saved him from certain death when being attacked by a grizzly bear. York was with the team when they arrived at the Pacific Ocean.

York helped negotiate relationships with Indians they met along the way. It seems they trusted him because of his black skin.

When the journey was finished, everybody was paid. Except for York. So, he asked for his freedom, he was turned down. He begged again so he could go back to Kentucky and be with his beloved wife.

And again, he was refused.

Instead, Clark sold him to a cruel task master and all information about "York the Slave" disappeared.

Today, a statue of York stands in Louisville, KY, a sad and unkind tale that shouldn't be lost to the digital dustbin of history.

His story matters.

Old Shoes

It seems to me, in many ways, an oil painting of shoes is about as difficult as doing one of the human hand. The curves, textures, reflection of light on leather, the precise nature of a shoe lace, shadow and light, perspective ... it seems so complicated.

Worn-out shoes were an unusual choice for Vincent. He found the old work shoes at a flea market then walked through the mud on purpose until they were filthy to make them interesting.

It was a dark, brooding painting much like those of his early years like the *Weavers* and *Potato Eaters*. This was painted in 1886, during a time of brilliant colors, thick paint and sunflowers. An odd addition to a brighter, more cheerful series of work.

He painted *"Shoes"* overtop another picture, a view from his brother Theo's apartment. He used the same canvas more than once on other occasions, too. It was a way of saving money.

Sometimes our lives are like that: we have to walk through the mud for a while to become interesting. The person we are now is painted over the person we used to be.

Vincent might have been crazy but he was instinctively wise.

*"I took a walk in the woods
and came out taller than the trees."*
Henry David Thoreau

124

Five Days

My father was an amazing man. He was respected and received many honors and awards for his bravery including the coveted Bronze Star. He was known for his passion, fighting spirit, the way he cared for and took care of his family, and his intense loyalty. He never gave up on anything.

After his years in the military he went to the police academy. He eventually became a detective in New York City and was one of the first in America to receive something called a car phone. His brother was a physician, and one day my dad noticed that his back was hurting more than usual. He was an athletic man, a physical person who loved exercise, fighting and hunting. But something was different, something was changing inside of him and he did not know what.

His health declined rapidly and a few months later, he was bedridden in a spare bedroom of his brother's house who tended my dad's declining health. Drugged up on morphine, my father died of cancer just five days before I was born.

Five days.

I was 12 when I found out about him. Much older when I discovered his life and family. I often wondered what it would be like to know the sound of my father's voice when he called my name. I wondered how he would feel to know I was named after him, or I named my own son MichaelB after him. I wondered what it would be like to have the presence of my father guiding me, teaching me, opposing me, praising my small accomplishments, going for a walk, playing catch, having him show me how to change the oil in a car, getting angry at him knowing that I could because he wasn't going anywhere.

I am so much different than what my father was like. As many parents do with kids who pursue the arts, he might have opposed my choices and it could have caused us to be alienated, at least for a while.

Damn. Five days.

He never got to see or hold his son. I have no memory of him, his life or his voice. I wish I did. Even so, I feel so grateful to know Melody, Rachel, MichaelB, Makayla and Caleb. I love being their father. I'm so grateful they do not know what it's like *not* to have a father who celebrates them, who loves them dearly and unconditionally.

Today, as I write this passage, I miss that scrappy kid who became a military hero and one of the most awarded detectives in New York City. He passed away too young, too soon.

He's in my thoughts often, he's with me every day. I look at my hands and see his blood running through them, I look in my children's eyes and see his reflection looking back. I often wondered how my adult life would've been different if I had known him.

Today, like so many other days, I really miss my father.

My son MichaelB the day I finally found my father's grave.

*"We sail upon different ships
but we share the same storm."*
MJ

A *Signature* Decision

There are a tremendous amount of wonderful tributes to Pete, his life, his career and the energy he and Toshi expended in making the community of our human race better.

He influenced so many. Of course, I created *WoodSongs* based in a large part on Pete and Toshi's public television program called *Rainbow Quest*. My last book, *WoodSongs 4* was written in tribute to the work ethic of Pete and Toshi, and it was dedicated to them. I encourage you to check it out.

Musically, I don't think I can contribute anything better to what Pete and Toshi meant than what many of my friends have already done. Pete's example impacted me as a boy growing up as his neighbor, even before I realized who he was. His was not so much a musical influence as it was an attitude. Pete's music and mine are very far apart, although planted in the same garden.

His vision of being a musical Johnny Appleseed is what inspired the creation of the *SongFarmers* community which has grown nationwide with nearly 100 chapters as of this writing.

I've been trying to think of a way to acknowledge the good example and inspiration of someone like Pete Seeger. Even the sloop *Clearwater* was a gargantuan effort for a folksinger to undertake and he did it by bringing together a community, making the cause more important than himself.

Of course, there's always the detractors: they will make politics and social issues supersede the good work of an honest musician who tried to live the reality of what he believed. That's OK, everybody has their own viewpoint.

I'm reminded of something Don McLean wrote to me once, saying people had to remember *"Pete sailed the Hudson river, he did not walk on it."* Don was one of the original sloop singers aboard the Clearwater, greatly influenced by Pete and the Weavers music, and that was quite a realistic and insightful comment on a great man. Don is right.

Anyway, considering how to acknowledge Pete's influence without diving into the myriad of tribute concerts and albums and becoming part of a well-meaning crowd, I decided to adopt his signature.

Pete's wife was of Japanese decent, a culture that often added art to the family names. Pete started doing that during the last third of his life, signing his postcards and letters with a little banjo alongside his name in tribute to his wife. He would also tape little leaves to his letters to add the idea of environmentalism to notes, often written on the backside of scrap paper.

So, to acknowledge his positive influence, I've decided to add that banjo to my own signature, a silent acknowledgment of the powerful example of a humble man who walked the walk and lived the life he believed in.

"I want to turn the clock back to when people lived in small villages and took care of each other."

"Participation is what will save the human race and I feel my whole life is a contribution."

Pete Seeger

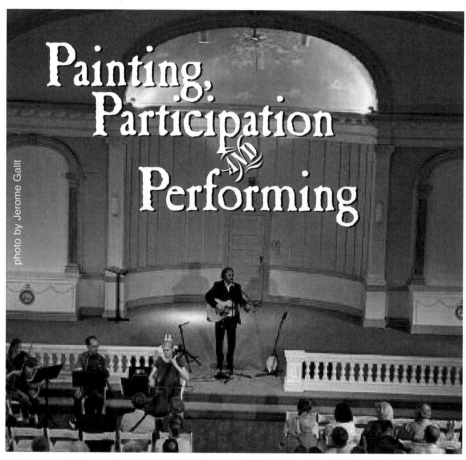

Painting, Participation and Performing

"If you hear a voice within you say you cannot paint, then by all means paint so that voice will be silenced."
Vincent van Gogh

There is a big difference between being a *participant* and a *spectator*. A participant helps make things happen, a spectator sits back and watches it unfold. You can still be a "fan" and stay a participant. Let's figure this out:

One of the greatest achievements of Vincent is he inspired so many others to paint. I don't know many folks who aspire to paint like Rembrandt, but thousands look at a van Gogh and think, *"I want to try that!"* The fans become participants. One of the greatest privileges of being a participant in life is that of being a parent. Another is being an artist. Both create and inspire. In theory, anyway.

Woody Guthrie has the van Gogh effect, folks hear his songs, the simplicity of them and think, *"I want to try and write like that."* Not many think *"I want to write like Beethoven,"* but hundreds of thousands across generations pick up a guitar and think they can write a song like Woody Guthrie.

Accessability causes Participation. Remember that in your work. Van Gogh, Guthrie, Dylan and others found success by being accessible, encouraging others to follow their footsteps, to get off the couch and try it.

Pete did the same by turning his audience into participants. He got them singing. He made them the "star." It is a great example where the audience became part of the song. The fans became the music. The audience became the concert. They became fellow participants.

And that is the great mistake of the music business when it was born almost 100 years ago. Someone learned how to capture vibrating air on plastic discs. But how do you market vibrating air on plastic to make the most money? Easy: Turn the audience from participants into mere spectators, convince them only stars are truly qualified to vibrate air and sell them on the idea for them to "participate" they must buy the vibrating air on plastic.

Music went from being created on front porches to artificial imprisonment on cylinders and then sold to an audience of spectators, not participants. Even worse, is the creation of the business model that to vibrate air, venues would have to pay licensing fees that may or may not be accurately distributed to the ones who created the vibrating air to begin with.

What I am most proud of with *WoodSongs* and the *SongFarmers* community is the grand audience is treated as fellow participants. They are not relegated down to simply spectators.

When you find yourself sitting back and watching, when you find yourself feeling like your music is not good enough, your songs are not good enough, that your living room couch has no value, that your front porch is silent … remember: you are being sold a business model of a dying enterprise.

The music business trained the audience to do nothing but pay for stuff. The music business trained the audience to simply be *ticket buying spectators.* They are now reaping the disaster of an audience used to doing nothing when it came to music. Now music is a tsunami of noise and free everywhere.

And when you read articles about the music industry moaning and complaining about this plight, remember: they did it to themselves. The only solution to the industry of music is to treat it, no longer as an "industry," but as a human right and privilege, something shared and treated as a gift.

> *"What's good about folk music is that it is not show business. Nor should it be."*
> **Pete Seeger**

Music can still be a commodity, an enterprise that feeds families and supports artists. But the business model has to be changed to be proactive and fit what is truly happening, the old business model should be discarded for something fresh and new that actually works and supports the artists willing to roll the dice to have a career in a beautiful art form.

The only business model that will truly work is when the chains that imprison music are broken and the artists become free to "vibrate air" wherever and whenever they choose in a way that will support those creating that vibrating air.

> *"If art is to nourish the roots of our culture, society must set the artist free to follow his vision wherever it takes him. We must never forget that art is a form of truth."*
> **President John F. Kennedy**

Henry David Thoreau, October and Art

It was 1862, almost two decades before Vincent began his painting career in Europe and almost two decades after Thoreau spent two years, two months and two days in a small $28 cabin along the shores of Walden Pond. The land was loaned to him by Ralph Waldo Emerson and Henry went there to write a book about his late brother, John. Instead, he left the cabin with several journals that had no story line whatsoever.

It took years before he could get the small book published, released to virtually no fanfare at all. Years after his passing, his unnoticed missive about the earth, nature and a simple life became legendary. *Walden* remains one of the most important works in American literary history.

As he lay dying in his family home in Concord, Thoreau worked to complete his final project – an essay celebrating the majesty of autumn, called *"October, or Autumnal Tints,"*

One of his most poetic, artistic passages is this:

"October is the month for painted leaves.
Their rich glow now flashes 'round the world.
As fruits and leaves and the day itself acquire a
bright tint just before they fall so the year near its setting.
October is its sunset sky."

Henry David Thoreau

Suicide
AND
UnFriending

"Out beyond ideas of wrong and right
there is a field of flowers.
I'll meet you there."
Rumi

Vincent and the Scottish art dealer Alexander Reid were friends. For a while, anyway. They had compatible life paths: Vincent was once an art dealer who became a painter, Alexander was a painter who later became an art dealer.

Here's where things get weird: they looked like twins. Really. They looked so much alike that van Gogh's portraits of Alexander were ofter mistaken as his own self-portraits. Scottish painter Archibald Standish Hartrick, who knew both personally, wrote of their remarkable resemblance in his memoir, *A Painter's Pilgrimage Through Fifty Years*. He wrote:

"The likeness was so marked that they might have been twins.
I often hesitated, until I got close, as to which of them
I was meeting. They even dressed the same."

Reid himself was an excellent artist as well as a gallery owner and the two friends often painted together.

As artists would often do, the friends would gift each other various canvases. Reid's father couldn't stand Vincent and sold a van Gogh still life, *Basket of Apples,* for just a few francs to get rid of it, calling the painting "newfangled French claptrap."

That small canvas was one of the first paintings where he would simply sign his first name, *Vincent.*

For a while the two were roommates and very close. Both stayed with Theo in Paris for nearly half a year. Both also struggled with depression and mood swings. Eventually, as with Paul Gauguin, the relationship darkened and fell apart.

At one point, as their friendship failed, Vincent proposed the two commit suicide together. Remember Vincent sneaking up on Gauguin with a knife? Here we go again. This completely freaked out Reid and he fled back to Scotland.

This angered Vincent and in a letter to Theo, he justified his rage and "unfriending his friend," ridiculing that Reid acted more like a businessman than an artist.

That painting of apples held in such distain by Reid's father? It's now worth millions.

A photo of Alexander Reid

Vincent's painting of Alexander Reid

Thou Shalt Believe

Sometimes, the most powerful fuel to drive any artistic endeavor forward is the unwavering belief from the artist who creates it. Some examples:

He knew in his heart what he was doing was right and, even though he only sold one painting in his lifetime, his work is now worth hundreds of millions of dollars.

Because Vincent believed.

Once upon a time, there was a 40 year old journalist in Boston who had a stroke and was told she had just six months to live. In 1916 she moved into the mountains of east Kentucky with her mother. A mountain man, Abisha Johnson, 55 years old with 7 children, had a dream she would teach his children to read. He crossed two mountains in a snowstorm, collapsed through her door and begged her to come to his holler. If she did, he promised to give her his land. Today his former land is the campus property of Alice Lloyd College.

Because Abisha believed.

Once upon a time there was a writer who didn't actually write novels or stories, he just liked to write about what he thought. No publisher wanted to release his books, few people ever read what he wrote. But he kept writing and writing and writing and writing because he loved what he was writing about. One day he was counting tree rings in the woods and it started raining and a few weeks later he died of pneumonia. A couple of decades later college students found a thin little book that was no longer in publication on the college library shelves and Henry David Thoreau became the most quoted literary giant in American history.

Because Henry believed.

Once upon a time, there was a young, mostly unknown movie director who had an idea for a film. He got the script and brought it to a studio for a low budget production that involved a fake fish. They agreed but offered hardly any money. The director told the studio, *"Your contract is virtually nothing, let's do this but I want 50 cents of every dollar over $50 million gross."* The studio bosses laughed, if a film did $25 million in those days it was huge and nobody believed a movie with a fake fish was going to gross $50M, so they said, sure we'll give you that. So the deal was made and *Jaws* grossed nearly $2 billion worldwide.

Because Steven Spielberg believed.

Steven had a friend who also liked to make movies. He had this crazy idea and convinced a studio to give it a chance. When the film was finished the studio bosses were horrified and considered the picture a colossal waste of money. When it came time to release the movie, they limited the picture to only 42 movie screens because the film was "doomed for failure" and they didn't want to invest anymore into it. But he insisted it would be a hit, and pushed and pushed until *Star Wars* went on to be one of the biggest grossing movies and brands in motion picture history.

Because George Lucas believed.

In the early 1960's, a young unsigned folksinger managed to get a review in the New York Times. Pop music was changing, Elvis was King and the Beatles were about to invade the world, so a kid with just a guitar was an unlikely investment for any major record label. But a producer had some clout, so Columbia Records gave it a shot ... and they spent all of $400 in one day recording an album deemed absolutely dreadful by the record label executives. It was so bad, selling only a few dozen copies, the project was nicknamed *Hammond's Folly.* But John Hammond believed ... and so did the young 20 year old kid. That album and the kid's career changed modern music forever.

Because John Hammond and Bob Dylan believed.

They are acknowledged as one of the greatest music groups of all time, but had a very rough go of it when they first came to America. With initial success in England, their record company refused to issue any of their music in the USA. When the label finally relented, a single was released but they completely misspelled the name of the band.

The single got no traction at radio and listeners even called stations asking them to stop playing that horrible song. After a lot of begging, Brian Epstein finally landed an appearance on a CBS variety show ... but very few people watched it because it was the same day that President Kennedy was shot. This new band from England was dead in the water. But they didn't give up, they tried again and have since become the most performed and revered band in modern music history.

Because The Beatles believed.

The lesson: never assume a stalled career is a statement of your value. You must believe.

Hope Matters

Hope is planting a seed
expecting to watch it grow.

Hope is choosing a path
others deny.

Hope is a banjo player
buying a tuner.

Hope is the first step
of a long journey.

Hope is posting on Facebook
believing others will see it.

Hope is loving a narcissist
believing they will change.

Hope is seeking truth
in an ocean of lies.

Hope is thinking what occurs in the dark
will be seen in the light.

Hope is wanting the truth to be stronger
than the lies that surround you.

Hope is believing a lie
because you do not accept the truth.

Hope is Art: creating what is not there
to portray a new reality.

Hope is writing about hope
hoping what you hope for
will be helpful.

Do You Hear What They Hear?

It was 1962. America was staring eyeball to eyeball with Russia as the Cuban missile crisis threatened the human race with nuclear annihilation. Students were practicing hiding under their school desks as though that would protect them from nuclear fallout. Families were building bomb shelters in basements and back yards. The world was on the edge of global war.

In New York City, a two songwriters were invited to write a holiday song ... but they couldn't, overwhelmed by the threat of unspeakable nuclear holocaust. In the studio they were glued to the radio every few minutes to see if war had started.

Noël was familiar with war, of German background and witnessed the horrifying aftermath of Nazi Germany. For a time he even served as a double agent in an effort to defeat Hitler.

Now in America, he and his wife, Gloria, turned to the calmness of the arts and music. But the world situation was overwhelming their creative sense.

Looking out the window of the recording studio, he saw two mothers pushing strollers on the sidewalk. The two children looked at each other and he saw them smile. The faces of those little babies, their innocence and their complete unawareness of the terrors around them, inspired his melody and his wife wrote his feelings with poetry.

Instead of a holiday ballad, they began writing a plea for help. In the lyric, the songwriters are essentially asking a tender question to those babies on the sidewalk:

"Do you see what I see? Do you see the missile heading our way? Do you see the nuclear fire heading our way?"

The lyrics were modified and tempered but the intent of the song was clear. They were afraid, alarmed and expecting war but wanting Peace.

The song was pitched as a simple holiday song, but it was actually an antiwar song. In the tune the child mentioned in the lyric is the child in the stroller he saw outside the recording studio window the day the world stared war in the eye.

It was a hard day in America. In a recording studio in New York City and the songwriting team of Noël Regney and Gloria Shayne Baker were worried along with everyone else.

It was 1962, and the world was on the brink of annihilation. Within one year President Kennedy would be assassinated and the Beatles would be heading to America.

Within one year Bing Crosby heard this song and agreed to record it ... and *Do You Hear What I Hear?* has became one of the most recorded holiday songs in history.

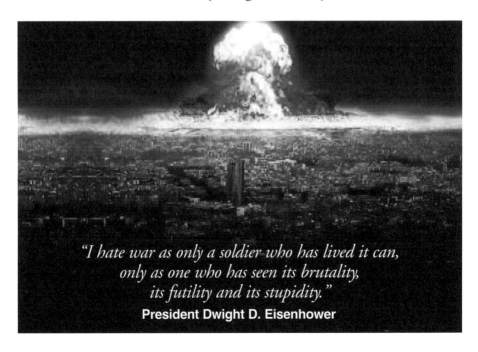

"I hate war as only a soldier who has lived it can, only as one who has seen its brutality, its futility and its stupidity."
President Dwight D. Eisenhower

The Mulberry Tree

He struggled with mental issues most of his life. In the spring of 1889, following a series of nervous breakdowns, he committed himself to an asylum in France. There his painting became more vigorous, his brushwork faster and paint thicker, a style worth tens of millions of dollars a century after he was gone.

The flaming colors of this painting called the *Mulberry Tree,* the deep shades of the sky and tree leaves are so thickly painted that the canvas surface almost becomes a sculpture. Vincent was excited with this painting, praising it in letters to Theo that he considered it his best.

Nobody liked it and Theo could not find a buyer. Vincent passed away just a few months later.

Copy-Cat

Almost psychotic in his work pace, Vincent poured out painting after painting during his last year of life. Weeks before his passing he continued a series of yellow drenched canvases imitating the work of other painters, as was his habit. This one is called *The Reaper after Millet,* one of dozens where he painted the poor, downtrodden, rural workers of France. He was interpreting a painting of the French artist Jean-François Millet.

I'm putting the two paintings side-by-side so you can see why Vincent's style troubled so many other artists. Their paintings were almost photographic in perfection, but Vincent was bold, cartoonish, distorted and untamed. Even so, he had no clue the style so many viewed as unprofessional would one day overshadow the work of all the "successful" artists of his day.

Millett painted like everybody else and today few know who he was. Vincent followed his original vision in spite of the professional condemnation, and transcended all of those so-called "good" artists of his day. That's the true value of critics, those who condemn the very things they themselves cannot do.

I always appreciate the words of Sibelius:

"Fear not the words of a critic, for no one ever erected a statue in honor of one."

Money-less Monet

The artist Claude Monet is considered the father of French Impressionism. He almost did not become an artist, instead signing up for the army ... until he changed his mind. His aunt purchased him out of the army to get his freedom.

He and his wife, Camille, lived in absolute poverty for most of his adult life. Creditors would often seize his paintings as payment for debt. Struggling to keep a home, he managed to buy a small boat which he converted into a floating studio. It was on this boat that he began painting his famous series of canvases, *the Water Lilies.*

He was a contemporary of Vincent, Renoir and others. Always broke, he used to beg the artist Renoir for loans to keep himself in paints and canvases.

By 1900, at sixty years old, his paintings started to become popular. Finally living out of poverty, his wife and son passed away and his health rapidly declined.

He completed over 2,000 finished paintings in his lifetime. Some were huge, 10 feet high and 30 feet wide. Monet struggled with depression, poverty and illness throughout his life. Aside from great personal loss, much of his depression was due to his increasingly failed eyesight. He died of lung cancer in 1926.

Lessons *of* Leonardo

Leonardo da Vinci, the most preeminent master of the European Renaissance and the king of art in 15th century Florence Italy, was born an illegitimate child. Considered the absolute lowest of the classes, the bastard child wasn't allowed to take his stepfather's name or enter into his business. Leonardo's last name was taken from the town he was born in, *Vinci.*

As a teenager, he knew he had to escape the class structure he was trapped in. He became an artist apprentice because, in Florence, artists were considered elegant members of the society. It was a step up from his bastard upbringing.

As an apprentice in the art studio he was able to study painting, sculpture and even engineering. All of this created the raging fire inside of him to escape the poor social class he belonged to. So obsessed to succeed, he would always dress impeccably to look important. He exercised a lot and it was said he could bend a horseshoe with his bare hands.

By 20 years old, he completed his schooling in the artist's workshop and received the coveted membership in the prestigious *Artist Guild of Florence.* Here is young Leonardo's very first painting, and when the art master of the studio saw the finished work, he never painted again.

Leonardo was obsessive about writing himself notes, so he always kept a notebook with him. He was left-handed, and as a boy learned to write backwards, from right to left. Scholars used to think this was some kind of code, thus the phrase *"da Vinci code."* He filled 15,000 pages in scores of notebooks of his thoughts, dreams, inventions and intentions.

Here's something I found interesting: the man hated painting, he did it mainly for the income. He struggled with keeping his focus, his mind was always racing with new ideas. Many scholars think he suffered from ADD or something similar. He was brought to court many times by benefactors angry with him because he did not finish the commissioned work.

His real love was engineering. To ingratiate himself with the local Duke, he sent the man a letter praising his own work as genius in military engineering. He designed what he called a "*covered war chariot*" and 400 years later it became the German tank during World War I.

It is only appropriate with his desire to be among the elegant, the world's most expensive painting is also by Leonardo.

In 1958 it was purchased for just $60 and it later sold for a staggering $450M. The work is called *"Salvator Mundi"* *(Savior of the World)* It was rediscovered in 2005, restored in 2007, then a Russian acquired the painting and put it up for auction in 2017. The price raced to $450 million after a telephone war between two bidders, won by Saudi Prince Bader.

From $60 to $450 million ... and today the ding-dang thing is missing. Amazing. Nobody knows where it is. I might start bidding for my paintings at $59 and see what happens.

"What am I in the eyes of most people? Somebody who has no position in society and will never have ... the lowest of the low."
Vincent Van Gogh

Ol' Blue Eyes

During World War I, this country had a strong dislike for Italians. There was an Italian family in Hoboken, NJ, tired of the prejudice they felt, so they made believe they were Irish and opened a little bar called the *Molly O'Brien Bar.*

The young son in that family really liked music, the crooning popstar of the day was Bing Crosby who mimicked the textures of jazz from a trumpeter named Louis Armstrong.

His experience as a young man hanging around bars, his father a guard for a bootlegging operation, and the tough streets of Hoboken followed him into his music career. He was a fighter. At the height of his career he was loved, feared and deeply respected. Both in albums, concerts and even in movies very few artists could even come close to his accomplishments.

He was one of the first modern singers to use a new invention in concert called a *microphone.* By the 1940s his career ascended the ranks of stardom so high that he decided to use his influence to correct many of the wrongs he saw.

Long before the *Black Lives Matter* movement, he made a public stand to support the idea of equality in race relations. In Harlem he discovered a trio of boys, the smallest one struck his fancy, and he began giving him opening act spots in his concerts.

The tiny little fellow who can dance up a storm was Sammy Davis Jr, and for the rest of his career Sammy would always credit Frank for supporting him at a time when a white performer supporting a black artist would have been the kiss of death for most careers.

In 1945, as World War ll raged on, Frank made a 10 minute film about race relations, prejudice and violence. So successful and influential was he that he convinced the music industry to doobie doobie do something no other artist would dare ask for: a record label just for himself called *Reprise Records.*

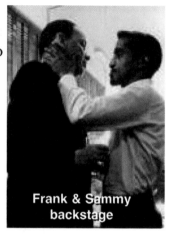

Frank & Sammy
backstage

Not exactly what you would call health-conscious, Frank would stop smoking and drinking for six weeks prior to recording an album or major concert appearances. He would stand in the washroom with a towel over his head by a sink with hot water pouring out of the faucet so the steam would clear his sinuses before he would perform.

Of all his many albums the one that I like the best is the 1966 recording of him in concert, his first live album called *"Sinatra at the Sands."*

The Yellow Man

During the final five years of his life, Vincent became obsessed with the color yellow. The bright, brilliant, comforting warm colors of the sun soothed his troubled soul. *"Yellow makes me happy,"* he wrote his brother Theo. *"It stands for the sun."*

As he descended into his troubled heart, Theo worried because many times Vincent tried to drink turpentine and eat his yellow paint. His depression often got so deep his doctors didn't think he could ever recover emotionally. He would bounce back, and his paintings would reflect his hope for brightness and joy. He always searched for the right yellow.

"There is a sun, a light that for want of another word I can only call yellow," he wrote. *"Golden citron. How lovely yellow is!"*

The problem with the yellow oil paints of his day is that, over time, the pigment is becoming brown and we are starting to lose the brilliance of Vincent's original vision on the canvas.

His painting below, simply called the *Mustard Field,* is another one of his less than appreciated efforts that display the magnificent colors of his amazing, yellow world.

He Was Only 35

He began his music career as a young teenager, studying and becoming very proficient at the clarinet. Exposed to rebels like James Dean and the social commentaries of Woody Guthrie, Pete Seeger and the Weavers, the young teenager began to explore the power of music.

It was during a visit to Florida, a young 18 year old Phil Ochs was jailed for horrible act of sleeping on a park bench. It was during his time in jail that he decided to become a writer.

He pursued studies in journalism at Ohio State, and while he was there was introduced to folk music through a friend. His political idealism became stronger while in college and he even started his own radical student newspaper.

By 1962, the folk boom was exploding across America and the epicenter was Greenwich Village, NY. He moved there and began writing songs that were embraced by the antiwar movement. Many of his songs were often topical, he would capture storylines from newspapers and magazines and the songs were ideally suited for what was happening at the moment.

Both a fan and competitor to Bob Dylan, they admired and irritated each other equally. Dylan liked the output and passion of Phil's songs, but grew tired of their political and social intensity. Phil had a habit of going out of his way to get on Bob's nerves, often successfully. It could best be described as mutual, friendly aggravation. One famous story is when they were driving together in Dylan's car, Bob threw Phil out saying he wasn't a songwriter, he was a journalist. Which was kinda true.

Deeply affected by the death of John F Kennedy, by 1968 the turmoil in America gave the protest singer a wealth of things to write about, but the assassination of Martin Luther King and Robert F. Kennedy weighed heavily on his emotions. He descended into alcoholism and depression.

Although popular among the singer songwriter and folk music circles, he never had an actual hit and was forced to live in the shadow of Bob Dylan which also effected his sense of place.

He tried changing his musical direction, working with a band on tour and wearing a gold suit which alienated many of his fans who were used to seeing him as a protest singer with just an acoustic guitar. His alcoholism became more intense and was compounded by the fact that he began taking drugs as well.

Depression, alcohol and drug abuse resulted in writer's block. He began to travel more in search of his muse. During one international trip he was jumped by robbers and during the attack was punched in the throat and which caused him to lose much of his vocal range.

By the mid-70s his behavior was becoming more erratic but his sense of social concern with still very strong. He tried to organize a benefit concert. When Bob Dylan found out very few tickets were sold and it looked like it would be canceled, he came to the aid of his friend and, when it was announced Dylan would perform that night, the event sold out quickly.

Managed by his brother Michael, Phil's decline of mental, emotional and physical health became more intense when he tried to change his personal identity. He took on a new name, *John Butler Train,* and claimed John killed Phil. His brother tried to place him in a psychiatric hospital at this point.

Suffering from bipolar disorder and alcohol abuse, in 1976 he moved in with his sister, Sonny. His life became limited to watching TV. One day, the depression, anxiety, drug abuse and alcohol coupled with bipolar disorder and the intense sadness of what he considered his failed career, he hung himself in his sister's home. She was the one who found him *(Sonny continues to work in folk music, she has her own radio program and is often seen on stage supporting artists at festivals.)*

Like many artists through time, his music was not really appreciated until he was gone. He wouldn't see how respected he would become, how precious his songs like *"I Ain't Marching Anymore"* and *"Love Me, I'm A Liberal"* would be viewed and how important he became in the canon of American music.

But still, he was only 35.

"I just can't keep up with Phil,
he just keeps getting better and better and better."
Bob Dylan

The Power of Light

During the early days of his painting career, about 1880 through 1883, most of Vincent's paintings were brooding and dark, reflective of the depressed areas that he lived in.

About 1885, Theo convinced Vincent to come to Paris where he had a gallery. There he was introduced to many of the impressionist painters of the day and learned the power of small dots and lines on canvas. He was overwhelmed by the power of light, the way sun reflected off mountains and water, the way the sunflowers bowed in obedience to the rising sun, all of this infused in Vincent an energy he had never experienced.

His canvases became bright, the color yellow becoming his favorite, believing yellow would bring joy to his own spirit. He began the habit of eating the yellow paint hoping to infuse himself with that same longed for joy.

He wrote to Theo he felt like he was a *"painting machine."* He was completing an average of three canvases a day, as if somehow he knew he was running out of time.

With the frantic nature of his painting, poor diet, drinking too much alcohol, gallons of coffee and smoking his pipe, his depression began to overwhelm him. It was at this time that he had a violent exchange with Paul Gauguin, threatening him with a knife and then running back to his small room and cutting off most of his ear.

Vincent voluntarily admitted himself into a hospital. Not just for depression ... he also wanted to save money because the expenses were so low. He soon moved to an insane asylum, struggling with seizures, explosive dreams and hallucinating. It was here he painted *The Starry Night.*

At the asylum he was kept mostly indoors, but as he recovered he was allowed to work back outside, and he began painting the light again.

He eventually moved to the village of Auvers-sur-Oise in France where he befriended an art lover who was also a physician, Dr. Gachet. Vincent liked the small town, the church that became one of his most famous paintings, and the wheatfields and cafes that surrounded where he lived. *Wheatfields with Crows* was thought to be his last painting, but lately that has changed.

Among the gardens within walking distance to his small apartment, he found an unusual clump of tree roots. He set up his easel and began to paint what would be the final work of his life, a lively and energetic painting called *Tree Roots*.

Something happened that day, assumed to be a suicide but lately it has been decided that two young boys shot Vincent by mistake and he refused to tell the authorities who they were. He made his way back to his small room and another boarder heard his groaning and sounded the alarm. His brother was summoned and Theo came to be at his side.

He had less than six hours left to live.

Renfro

A fellow named John Lair created a live audience radio broadcast that, for a time, was bigger than Nashville's *Grand Old Opry*. The show started at WLS in Chicago, then moved to WLW in Cincinnati. He was deeply committed to his boyhood home in Renfro Valley, so in 1939 brought the program home to Kentucky. Produced in an old barn, it was a precursor to *A Prairie Home Companion*, filled with stories and skits.

WoodSongs exists in the shadow of the legacy of the *Renfro Valley Barn Dance, Rainbow Quest*, the *Grand Ole Opry*, the *Louisiana Hayride* and others. It is a grand tradition, and we are proud to be part of it. When I created the show I wanted to focus on the artists, their backstory and the music. WoodSongs has a personality all its own.

I have to admit, to create a live audience anything that is produced early on a Monday evening in a rural community like ours in Kentucky is a downright miracle. What John Lair pulled off far away from any media center is a spectacular achievement.

Here's a piece of history: a photo of John's actual scripts from one of his Saturday broadcasts. WoodSongs owes a huge debt to Renfro valley ... and we should be very proud of the artistic community Kentucky has given birth to.

WoodSongs has produced over 1000 live audience shows. The new season of PBS and RFD-TV launches with new shows for them.

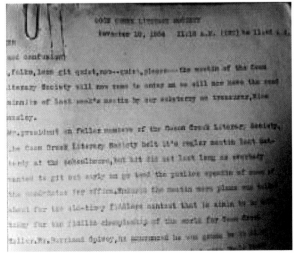

I enjoy gathering with our friends on Mondays, I love seeing the audience, the artists and the excitement of the lights-camera-action part of it.

The *Renfro Valley Barn Dance* is an important part of America's musical legacy. It is not on the air anymore, and I hope it does not evaporate in the digital dustbin of history.

We need to remember all the things that made our musical front porch so wonderful.

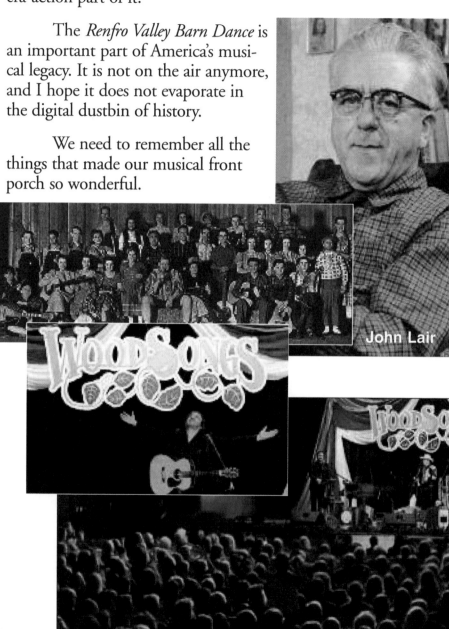

John Lair

156

The true tale of
Banjos,
Brooklyn Protest Marches
and
Bottled Water

It was a dad thing ... Melody was moving from New York City to Denver, and I was going to drive a cargo van from Lexington to Newport News, Virginia to NYC to Denver, Colorado and then back the Lexington. All in five days.

I rented the van in Lexington and drove it to Virginia to spend an evening with Rachel and MichaelB. We grilled out and watched movies and had a wonderful time together.

About noon the next day I got back into the van and drove seven hours north to New York City to meet Melody in Brooklyn, pack up all her stuff and begin the drive across the country to her new home in Denver. Nice easy plan.

Everything about the drive to New York City went fine, traffic was light and the weather was clear. I was making good time ... right up until the point I got to the edge of Brooklyn.

Listening to WCBS-AM radio I learned there was a massive protest march, thousands of people gathering around the Brooklyn Bridge, the very route I needed to take to get to Melody's apartment.

Both directions on the bridge were blocked and I was redirected to the nearby Manhattan bridge instead. On the cumbersome and slow trek to the Manhattan Bridge, literally thousands of people, mostly young people of color were gathering in peaceful protest to events going on around the nation.

As I got close to the Manhattan Bridge I realized it was also blocked by protesters, the police even barricaded the entrance to the bridge and I was stuck, no way to get to Melody and no way to turn around.

An Officer was nearby on the sidewalk so I called out to him, saying I was from out of state and trying to get to Gold Street, did you have any ideas how I could get there?

"Why are you in New York City?" he asked.

I told him I was from Kentucky, I played the banjo and proceeded to tell him about my daughter and needing to load up her stuff and get her out of the city and move her to Denver.

"Well the bridge is blocked and you're stuck here and it will take at least a couple of hours until the protest march moves out of the area," he said.

Well, pickles. I called Melody and told her the situation. Looking out the window, I saw the officer sweating profusely from all the stress and activity, so I rolled down my window and said,

"Would you like a bottle of fresh mountain spring water from Kentucky?" I reached beside me and took out a bottle of WoodSongs Highbridge Spring Water, and handed him the bottle which he gladly and gratefully accepted.

Looking at the bottle he asked, *"What is a WoodSongs?"*

I proceeded to tell him about the live audience broadcast in a beautiful theater in Lexington Kentucky and the 500 affiliate radio stations on PBS from Los Angeles to Vermont on the RFD television network coast to coast and American forces radio network in 177 nations and every single military base in the world, and schools across the country.

"That's my name above the WoodSongs logo," says I. So he calls out to his fellow officers, *"This fellow is from Kentucky and he plays the banjo and he's on TV."*

The other officers gathered around so I offered all of them a bottle of fresh Kentucky mountain WoodSongs 1000th Broadcast Highbridge Spring Water sitting next to me in the van.

They commiserate with each other as they're holding their Spring Water amidst the massive protest march going on in the streets nearby, one of them points to another officer who hops on his motorcycle. They remove the barricades to the Manhattan Bridge, looked at me and said:

"Go get your daughter and drive safe."

The officers opened up the barricades and the policeman on the motorcycle escorted me and my cargo van across the bridge, I loaded Melody's belongings up with the help of some of her friends and we went on our way to Denver.

This is a photo I took from my driver's seat of the police, the barricades and the gathering numbers of protest marchers.

The Masked Melody

I picked up Melody in New York City and began the long drive across the country to her new home in Denver, Colorado. It was a wonderful trip and I treasured every moment spending time with this amazing young woman that I get to claim as my baby girl.

Of course the ding dang Covid problem made certain things a little awkward, and such was the case when we stopped to fuel up at a roadside gas market. We pulled to the pump and Melody went inside to get a cup of coffee. Once the tank was full I went inside to get my usual bottle of Naked Juice.

As I entered the store, this woman in a mask walks out, confronts me and asked if I locked my van. Locked my van?

"Yes," says I. *"Why?"*

Abruptly, the strange, masked woman thrusts her hand out and says, *"Give me your keys."*

"I'm not giving you my keys, lady ... that's my van." The woman pulls her mask down and Melody says,

"Dad, it's me. What's wrong with you?"

Oh, yes... fatherhood at its finest.

I drop off Melody in Denver and spend a couple of delightful days with her. Now heading back home to Lexington, I am motoring through the long, straight and boring highways of Kansas at 5 AM. Lights start flashing behind me and I pull over to discover I was going 11 miles an hour over the speed limit. The police officer comes to my passenger side window as protection from the interstate traffic, I roll it down and he says:

"Care to guess?"

So I get humble and apologize. He asked what I was doing out this early in a rented cargo van? So I proceeded to explain the road trip from Lexington, Kentucky to Virginia to New York City to Denver when he stopped me:

"You were in New York this weekend during the marches?"

"I sure was…" And I proceeded to tell him the story of getting stuck in Brooklyn surrounded by thousands of peaceful demonstrators, caught on the Manhattan bridge and the kindness of the police officers as they let me across to scoop up my daughter and get her to Denver, and I was just now heading home to Kentucky.

"All that in four days? That's amazing. Can you prove it?"

So I pulled out my iPhone and opened up my Facebook page and showed him the story with the photograph of the officers waving me on at the base of the Manhattan bridge. He scans through the story and says,

"Do you really play the banjo?"

So, I tell him about the live audience broadcast on the 500 radio stations blah blah blah when he thrusts out his hand with my drivers license and says:

"Well, if New York can help you out I guess the Kansas police can, too. It was only 11 mph over so … drive slower. After all, if you play the banjo, I guess you need a break."

I thanked him politely, trying not to bust a gut from laughter. He was incredibly nice and friendly and I am very grateful to the Kansas state police for letting me come home with my bank account intact.

'nuff said.

Creations, Creatives
and a
Creator

"I cannot help thinking that the best way of knowing God is to love many things. Love this friend, this person, this thing, and you will be on the right road to understanding Him better."
Vincent Van Gogh

Rembrandt struggled with his art during a time when Christianity merged with Pagan practices. It opened up his art. Recently, I read a lot of stories about artists seeking a spiritual meaning for their work. Fear and pandemics often turn folks to God, and I suppose anything that directs people to a calm faith is probably a good thing.

I have a lot of agnostic and atheist friends and I often will engage in discussions on how they feel. There's no doubt in my mind that some of them will be quite energetic and vocal about why I am "wrong" for thinking the way I do.

That's fine, I enjoy the interaction and it often simply confirms my outlook. Most of the time people with opposite views from mine are shaped by great anger and disappointment.

I get it. That confirms my distrust of *religion* ... not of a Creators existence. My belief that there's a Creator should be stronger than a Facebook meme or somebody else's opinion.

The way I see it: something created this thing called life. Something created the organization and sensibility of it all. Something created what can only be described as the brilliance of the universe, the alignment of stars against the earth, the majesty of the interconnected cycles of our world.

Creation is complex and organized. Life is planned and brilliant. The lens of your eye is impossible to duplicate, your finger prints are unique and your heart is incredibly designed. It is unthinkable for one, no less all, of this to simply "happen."

I think the greatest validation a God exists rests in the reasoning of people who doubt God exists. The fact that you can take inanimate molecules and assemble the inanimate matter into a living, intelligent being with the power to question the existence of what turned the inanimate molecules into the living being is proof enough that a creator exists.

To me, anyway.

So it is in the world of music and art. I can't claim to understand it, I just know I love it. I need it. I want it and in my spirit I am driven to create it. In that regard, I understand a higher power, a Creator, and it makes sense that I would be designed in that same image. I don't feel acceptance of a Creator has to be religion based. Religion is essentially a man-made creation with man-made traditions that are more often than not contradictory if not irrelevant.

And I also don't think it's necessary to understand everything about a Creator either. Doubt, in and of itself, does not disprove anything. *Lack of understanding,* in and of itself, does not disprove anything.

Most men do not understand women ... that does not mean women do not exist.

Thank God.

*"God sends us pieces of art so
that we may see ourselves in them."*
Vincent van Gogh

Hank History

The often troubled, depressed and alcoholic Hank Williams became a hugely popular country music superstar after World War II.

His first marriage to Audrey, Hank Jr's mom, failed and his life tumbled in a cloud of drinking. He soon met a young 19 year-old girl, Billy Jean and married her during a late-night ceremony after Hank performed his set on *The Louisiana Hayride.*

Worried his first wife would show up and cause a scene, they got married privately, but to raise money Hank decided to remarry her at a sold out, ticketed concert with over 10,000 people attending. It worked out so well that the eternally broke Hank decided to do it yet again, another ticketed event to remarry the same young girl.

A little over a year later, with his rapidly declining health, he died on the way to his final concert on New Year's Day in 1953.

His body was at his mothers boarding house for two days and visited by Joe DiMaggio and his wife Marilyn Monroe. A day later, January 4, over 25,000 people attended the public memorial and funeral.

Unmatched by any country artist before or after, Hank Williams was only 29 years old when we lost him.

John's Broken Thumb

In 1970, Bill Danoff of the *Starland Vocal Band* was the soundman for a small folk club near Washington DC. On New Year's week they were hosting an up-and-coming songwriter that performed there previously with other groups, a very energetic fellow named John Denver.

After one of the concerts Bill invited John to his basement apartment with friends to pass a guitar and other substances around. John didn't show up and they got worried so they tracked him down. It turns out Denver got into a car wreck and was in the hospital. He was OK, but he unfortunately smashed his hand into the windshield and broke his thumb.

Back at Bill's apartment, the always energetic John Denver still wanted to pass the guitar around even though he couldn't play. One of the songs suggested was Bill's unfinished tune that mentioned a state he never set foot in,

West Virginia.

The song was originally intended for Johnny Cash but they did not know Johnny Cash nor did they have any connections that would lead this song his way. That night they finished the song and three days later went into a studio to record it.

Bill Danoff & John Denver
Photo courtesy of the Dominion Post

When you hear *(Take Me Home) Country Roads*, that is Bill playing the acoustic guitar because John Denver had a broken thumb. The song eventually became a massive hit for Denver, and was recorded by hundreds of others.

The Good Lesson of
Mr. Rogers

"Listening is where Love begins."
Mr. Rogers

He had a bachelor's degree in music, so he understood its gentle power. He also became a minister, so he understood the respect for the gift of art. And families. And children.

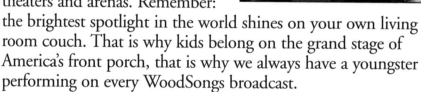

Music is indeed a spectacular gift, it is the soundtrack of America's front porch. In a noisy angry world, music gets people to stop fighting ... and to listen. You cannot fight, you cannot argue when you're listening. That makes music the greatest expression of love in human history. It makes musicians the biggest peacekeeping force in the world.

It doesn't have to be in theaters and arenas. Remember: the brightest spotlight in the world shines on your own living room couch. That is why kids belong on the grand stage of America's front porch, that is why we always have a youngster performing on every WoodSongs broadcast.

I always wanted to do a spin-off show, like *WoodSongs*, only it would exclusively feature kids. Maybe set on a front porch, sort of *Mr. Rogers meets the Grand Ole Opry.*

*T*he Cool *of the* Day

To me she was a musical goddess of Appalachian music. She was sweet, kind and always encouraging. When I started WoodSongs she was one of the very first major artists to jump on board and be supportive.

But my friendship with Jean and her husband George started long before the broadcast did. Two years earlier I decided to write my first book, *WoodSongs One.* I envisioned it sort of like the Foxfire series, several books that, as a whole, would tell a huge story. And here we are with *WoodSongs 5,* none of it would be here without Jean Ritchie.

I had writers block. I knew what I wanted to write but it just wasn't coming. I was performing a concert in eastern Kentucky with her, Jean told me that she had a family log cabin in Viper, just outside of Hazard. I was welcome to stay there for a weekend and see if that would energize my creativity.

I did and it worked. The book was done and the album was planned. When it came time to record Homer Ledford, JD Crowe, Odetta and other friends jumped in to help. Jean agreed to play a solo rendition of *Shady Grove* on her mountain dulcimer for me as part of the album.

Our friendship expanded when I moved to Winchester and got to know Homer and Jean's wonderful sister, Edna.

Jean Ritchie was the Princess of Appalachia, the *Mother of Folk Music.* Over the course of her career she performed with the great folk artists of the 20th century like Woody Guthrie, Bob Dylan, Pete Seeger, Joan Baez, Leadbelly and many others. Born in the hollers of the Appalachian mountains she traveled the world with her mountain dulcimer.

The last time I saw her, I had breakfast with Jean and her talented husband George. He told me the story of how he would make his wife's dulcimers in his little workshop and Jean would talk about her home in Long Island, New York.

Sometime after her passing we did a tribute show to the music and career of Jean Ritchie and it was very nice to have her son Jon Pickow part of the broadcast. He has since passed away.

Photo by Larry Steur

Jean embodied the music and spirit of Appalachia and the joy and heartache of mountain music. Her song *Cool of the Day* is a brilliant reflection of life in the mountain hollers, her book, *"Singing Family of the Cumberlands"* remains a classic. She represented her community with grace and dignity.

She's the foundation bedrock for the music of America's front porch and I am beyond grateful I was able to know her.

"I have never been able to decide which times I liked better, those winter evenings around the fireplace, or the summertime twilights on the front porch. I was doing my share singing to the moon on those soft summer nights."
Jean Ritchie

My Old Brown Earth
(Ma Vieille Terre Brune)

It wasn't until I was almost finished with the painting that I realized what it was actually about: Pete has a tender song called *"My Old Brown Earth,"* a sensitive song about his own impending passing. It has become the title of this oil painting.

I did not understand why everything in the painting was so symbolic, mystical and, well, brown. Why was I leaving Pete as an undefined silhouette? The painting reflects his love for the Hudson river, the Clearwater, his banjo without his slogan on it, he's singing but to no audience. Even the flowers become red white and blue.

I won't explain what the symbolism in the painting means to me personally, you can have your own interpretation, assuming it's something that you care to dwell on.

Anyway, the song (found on the *Pete* album) inspired this painting. The lyrics of the song are a bit startling, he is singing about his own impending death, a reality for us all to face.

Someday.

His *someday* finally came January 27, 2014. I'm sure I will tweak it here and there, minor touches as the oils dry but essentially the painting is done.

"I'm not afraid of death;
I just don't want to be there when it happens."
Woody Allen

Social Media, Public Shaming
AND
Vincent

"Ridicule is mankind's most potent weapon."
Saul Alinsky, 1934

Vincent's genius was fueled by a lifetime of complete rejection. I think that is part of his legend, his allure. His burning ambition to present his art to the common man was ridiculed by the establishment, shunned by his contemporaries and rendered valueless by the patrons of his day.

That afternoon, van Gogh set out for the wheat fields where he had recently been painting a grand canvas of the same name. This day, he worked on a painting called *Tree Roots*.

On the evening of July 27th, 1890 he returned to the Auberge Ravoux Inn in the village of Auvers-sur-Oise in northern France where he lived holding his bleeding stomach.

It took nearly 20 hours of bedridden agony, but by early morning July 28th he died of a single gunshot wound to the belly. His brother Theo and Dr. Gachet were at his side.

Understanding what was happening at the time of his passing will break your heart.

The local folks, headed by the town grocer, drafted a petition calling for Vincent to be interned in a mental asylum as a danger to women and children. Kids

Dr. Gachet's sketch of the dying Vincent

threw stones at the ragged, red-bearded painter with staring eyes. The mayor soon had Van Gogh committed to a padded cell in the hospital. Vincent was, in a word, humiliated.

> *"We the undersigned, residing in the city of Arles, Place Lamartine, have the honour to inform you that the man called Vincent, landscape painter, a Dutch subject, living in the aforementioned place, has for some time in various ways shown that he does not enjoy his full mental abilities, and that he is given to an excess of drink, after which he is found in a state of overexcitement such that he is no longer aware, neither in fact, nor in speech, and is very worrying for all residents of the quarter, and mainly for the women and children."*

I wondered what it would have been like for Vincent if this happened in the age of social media.

Brutal, I would think.

Recently, somebody sent me a screenshot of a post where I was mentioned in the context of ridicule over something I was not even involved in, making fun of my interest in Thoreau and van Gogh's work was the basis of the ridicule.

Did it bother me? No, I don't even know this person. Never met them, never had a conversation and they know absolutely nothing about what I think or feel about anything. It was just a public slam on a thread that was nothing but slamming other people.

It is a fact: if you are a musician, artist or someone who thinks outside the box ... those trapped inside the box are going to try to pull you back in. It's a tiny, small minded, sad little world when the greatest creative output of your time on earth is used to degrade others doing what you are incapable of doing.

"Fear not the words of a critic,
for no one ever erected a statue in honor of one."
Johan Sibelius, 1949

There was a time when these things would bother me. Social media has become a vicious, fierce weapon where inactive people vent their personal humiliations upon those trying to accomplish something worthwhile. That's true of the arts, literature, poets and, yes, even politicians. No one can escape the bloody, digital claw of social media.

"Great minds discuss ideas;
small minds discuss people."
Eleanor Roosevelt, 1955

Of course these quotes were made well over half a century ago, before Facebook, Twitter and other digital platforms invaded the consciousness of our culture. What started out as a great idea has become a horrific weapon in the hands of people incapable of understanding the damage they cause.

Unkindness is often very loud.

Innocence is best reflected in silence. Someone told me a long time ago, *"always let somebody else be the last stupid sound in the room."*

Never respond, certainly not publicly, to those reflecting their own foolishness with harsh words about you, or anyone else for that matter.

The true sadness is what happens to those who are innocent. The bloody bruises and public damage that can happen to someone who is the victim of public shaming, projection, narcissistic digital blasting can be painful to overcome. It can be impossible to recover from it. It can be very difficult to even maintain your personal calmness. The natural reaction is to respond. To defend. To stand on a rooftop and scream to the world, "these idiots don't have a clue what they're talking about!"

> *"A lie can travel half way around the world*
> *while the truth is putting on its shoes."*
> **Mark Twain, 1903**

I am using these quotes from respected authors and historic personalities to give a little comfort to those who have been victims of this unsavory behavior. "Stupid" has been around a long time, "gossipers" have been inflicting their damage for a long time.

What happened to Vincent is not new.
What is happening to you now is not new.
And you are not alone.

You can identify an idiot by the incessant noise they make. They suck in the weak minded and especially those bored with their own lives into their dismal vortex of angst. They are a source of supply for those riddled with insecurity and they form a loud but tiny community that accomplish absolutely nothing.

They will even try to weaponize someone you care deeply about in an effort to ruin your reputation, to meddle in your life, to even devastate how you make a living to support your family. They are narcissistic neanderthals.

If someone you love is caught in the clutches of these insignificant bloodsuckers, hold your ground. Keep your dignity. Never be affected by the gaslighting and slander, it can be so vicious that you yourself might even start believing it's true.

Strength is reflected in your quiet dignity. By responding to social media gossip, you lower our own self into the digital cesspool these bottom feeders live in.

I am writing this because these days most people are isolated, bored. They seek anything that will fill the hours with some kind of focus or excitement. Many will lean toward the negative, the harsh, they will want to inject themselves into what they perceive is the good life of someone else. They will want to validate their failures by tearing down what they see as a good thing.

Someone said that they felt my message about America's front porch was like listening to a *snake oil salesman.* That hurt. Just for a minute. And then I realized how sad for that person, how empty their heart and soul must be that they could take something good and drag it down into the black hole their spirit is trapped in. So be it, in the end it does not matter.

Remember Vincent, the failure. During his brief career he sold just one painting. A century after he painted it, his *"Portrait of Dr. Gachet"* sold at auction for a record-breaking $82.5 million. The price remains one of the highest ever paid for a painting.

·The Painter

And so here we are. The book is finished, my tribute to art, music love & family written in the spirit of Vincent and those that inspired and affected me to become a musician, song-writer and artist.

When that darned pandemic hit, I had to decide how to best use my time. All touring stopped. The business of music stopped. But, art is born of isolation, so during that isolated, quiet time, an artist supposedly should do their best work, right?

So I turned my attention to oil painting and studied the artists I admired, and settled quickly on Vincent. He is to the art world as Woody Guthrie and Bob Dylan are to the music world. As a folksinger I get what makes their music so needed. Besides the power of their lyrics, it's the accessibility of their songs. They're simple, everybody wants to play them. I wanted my work to feel just as accessible. That is why I used van Gogh, Seeger, Thoreau and others as mentors, not to copy them, but to be inspired. In the absence of a father, they became my teachers.

Painting inspired me to write the songs for the album, a song cycle about art, music, love and life. The title cut is also the theme song of the ongoing work for a movie script I am writing of the same name, *The Painter*, about Vincent coming back today to see his despised work now celebrated worldwide. How would he feel? How would he react? It makes for an amazing story.

For me, the title song, *The Painter*, is about the idea of the blank canvas of life being filled with all the colors of life. Art, music, painting, family, love, loss and the energy of seeking the next moment, the next thing. Writing these songs was exhilarating and painful all at the same time.

The title song is a derivative of the classic *Vincent (Starry, Starry Night)*, the two songs act as bookends on the album. *Blues Tonight* is the most fun to play, I like the guitar part. The timely plea of *The Statement* is balanced by Harry Chapin's *Cats In The Cradle*, embellished by a hammer dulcimer. Dylan's plaintive *Make You Feel My Love* is written in the colors of love. *Vincent In The Rain* creates the imagery of Vincent's search for love in France and viewing the love of your life as a masterpiece, while *Othello* merges the deception in the Shakespeare play with the idea of the deception of a blank canvas, creating what was not there.

As for the CD cover, I chose to paint one myself in the spirit of what the book, the album and movie script was about. After all, how hard can it be to paint like Van Gogh?

Well, it's pretty ding-dang hard :)

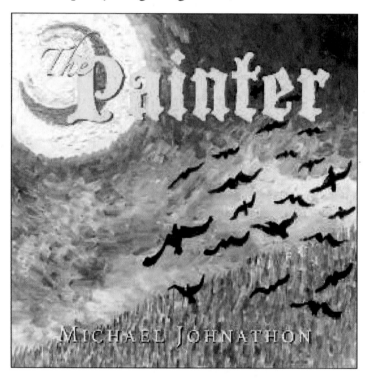

For a digital download of The Painter album, visit MichaelJohnathon.com/ThePainterCD

As a bonus track to the official release, the song *Legacy* is included in the attached CD album. It is a 9-minute roller coaster about the world of folk music, from Pete Seeger to the collapse of the record industry. Like Vincent, we all have a long, long way to go.